Build It!

Make Supercool Models with Your Favorite LEGO® Parts

WORLD LANDMARKS

Jennifer Kemmeter

GRAPHIC ARTS BOOKS®

Contents

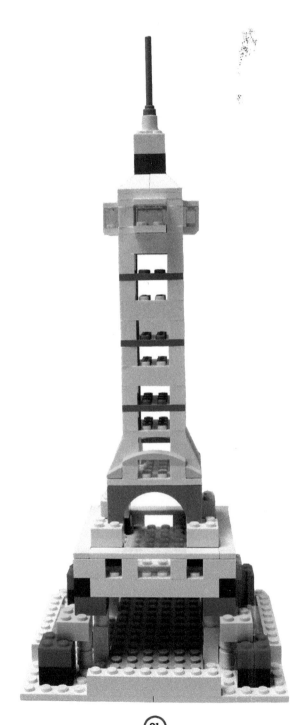

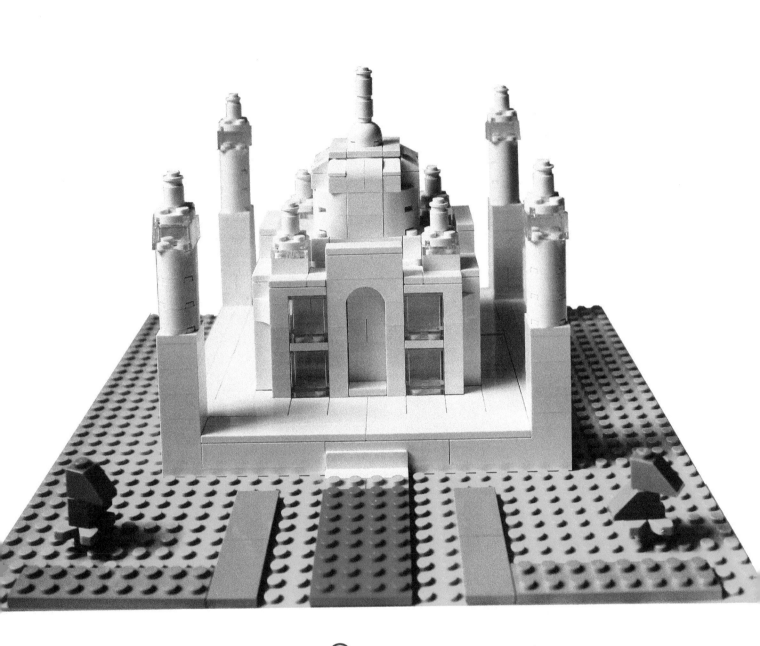

38

The Taj Mahal

How to Use This Book

An illustration of the finished Eiffel Tower that looks like the pictures in the steps.

What you will be building.

A photo of what your finished Eiffel Tower will look like.

Build the Eiffel Tower

A picture of each piece you will need.

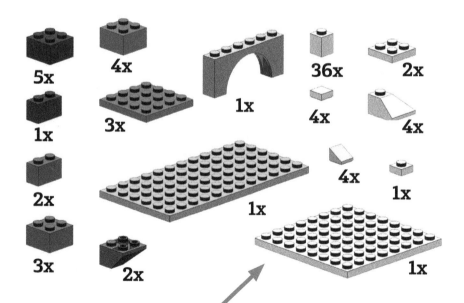

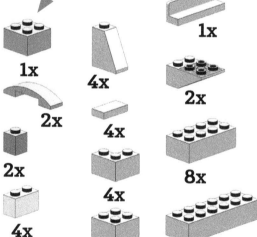

5x

4x

1x

3x

2x

3x

2x

1x

36x

4x

2x

4x

4x

1x

1x

1x

2x

4x

2x

4x

4x

12x

1x

4x

2x

8x

2x

All the pieces you will need to build the Eiffel Tower are listed at the beginning of each of the instructions.

4

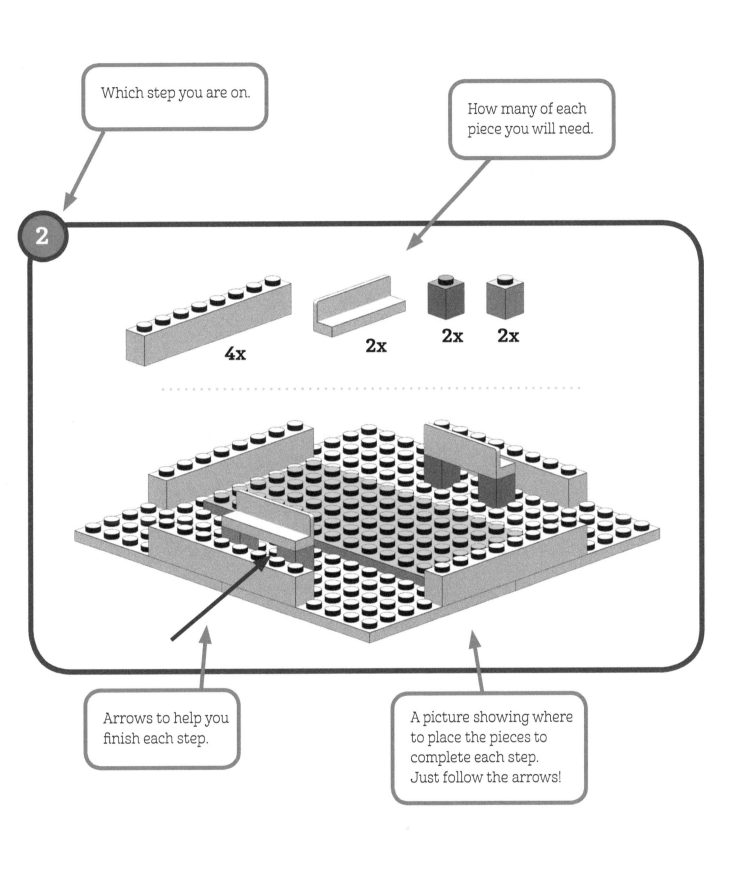

Which step you are on.

How many of each piece you will need.

2x 2x 2x 4x

Arrows to help you finish each step.

A picture showing where to place the pieces to complete each step. Just follow the arrows!

The Empire State Building

Build the
Empire State
Building

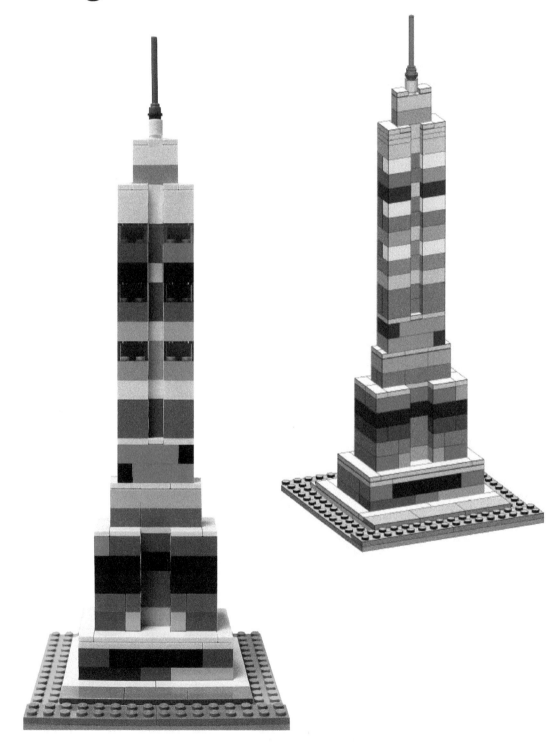

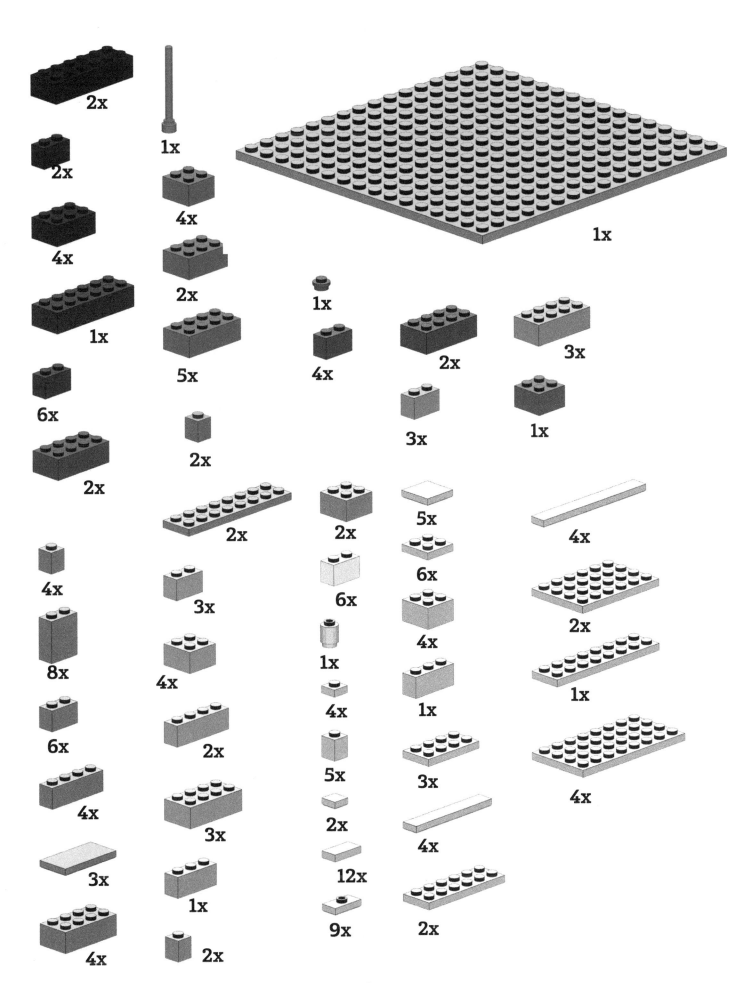

9

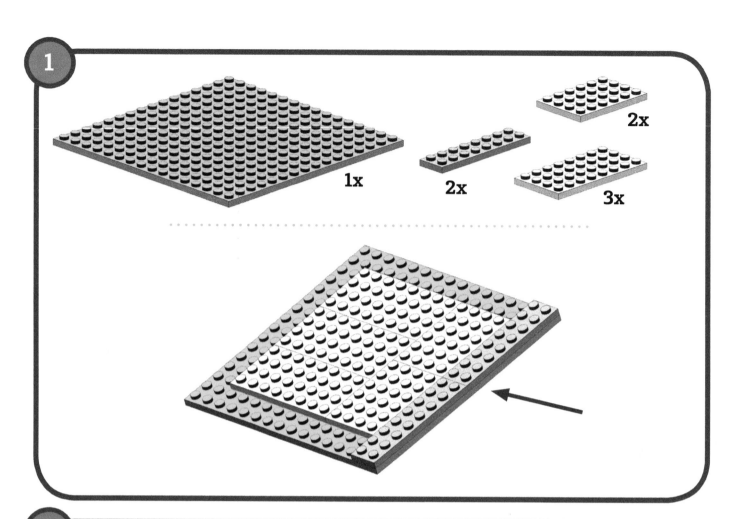

1x 2x 2x 3x

2x 2x 5x 3x

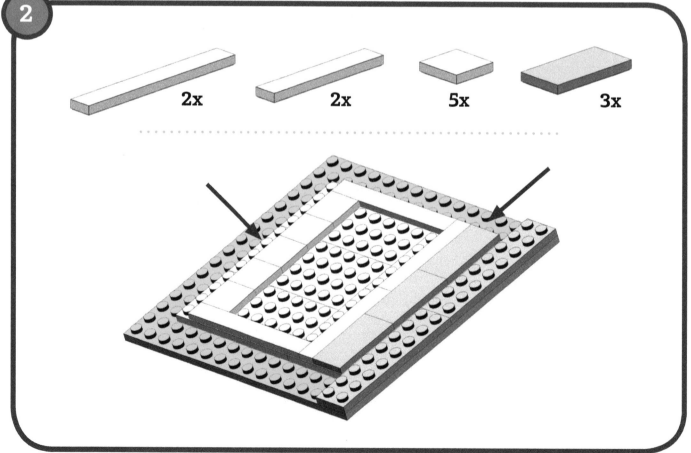

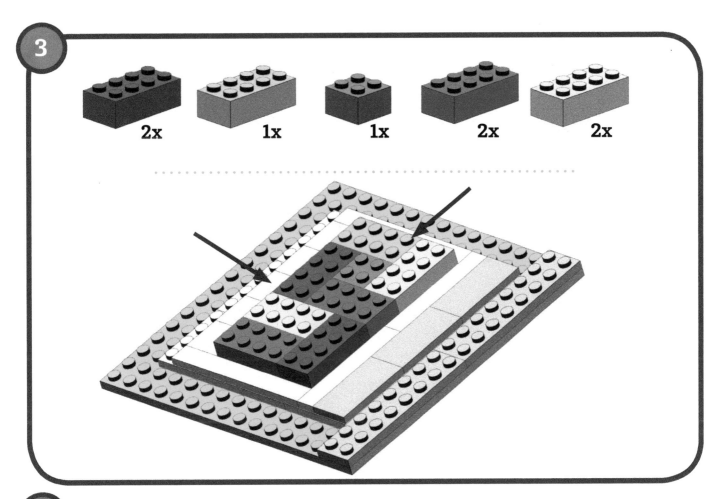

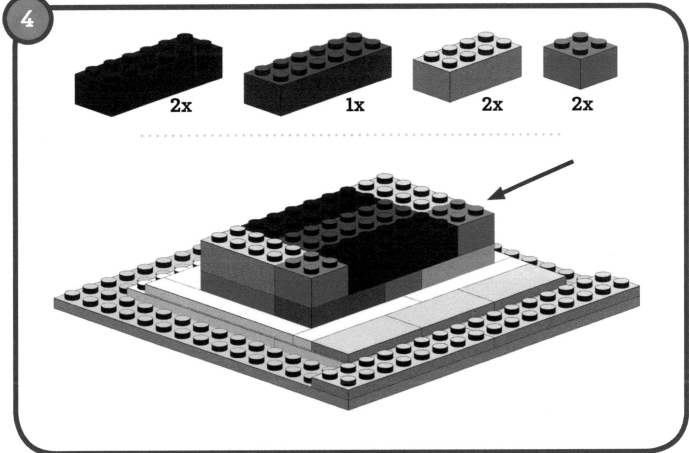

5

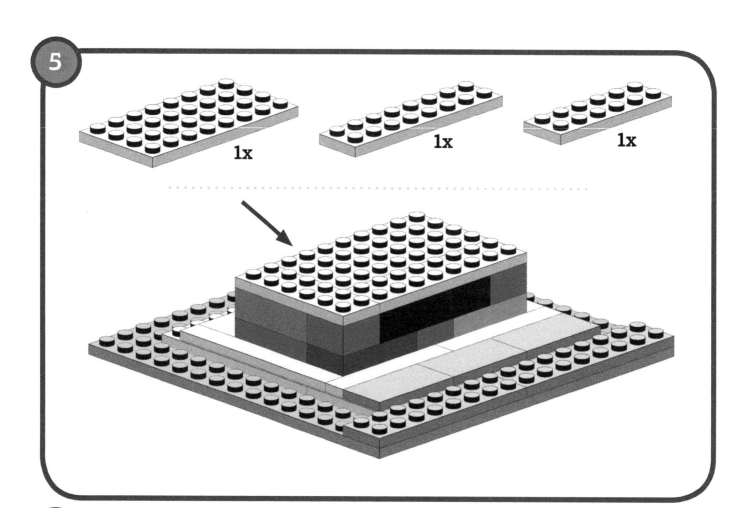

1x   1x   1x

6

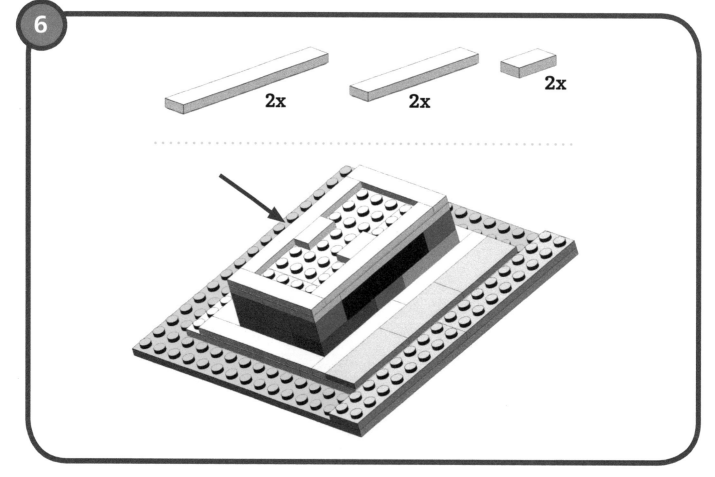

2x   2x   2x

7

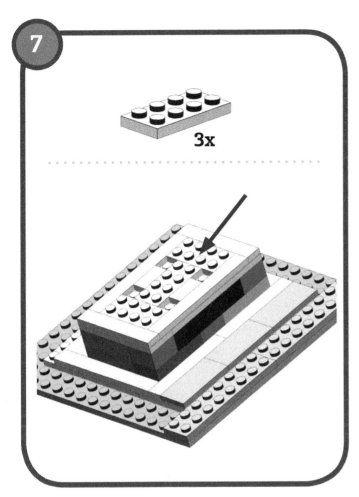

3x

8

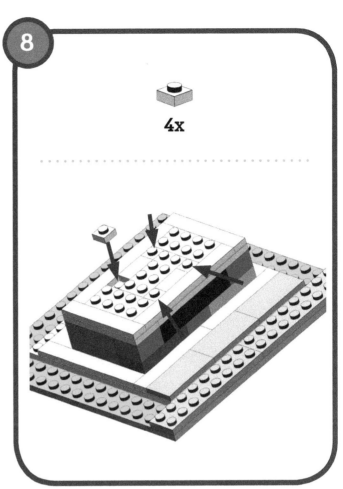

4x

9

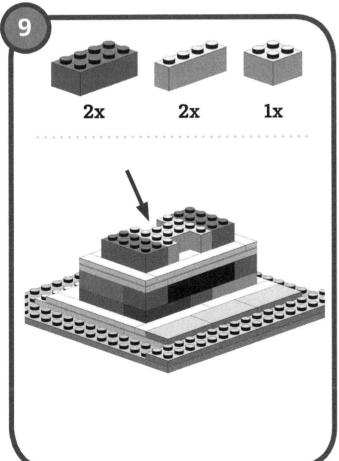

2x   2x   1x

10

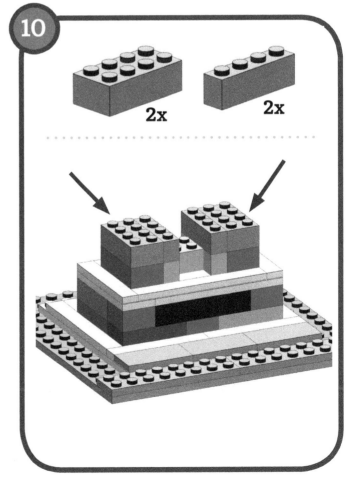

2x   2x

13

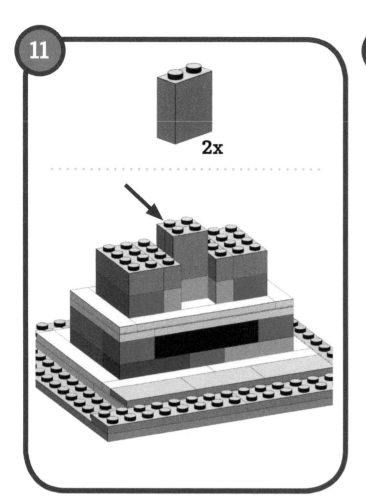

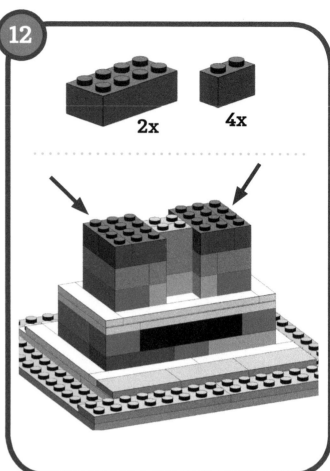

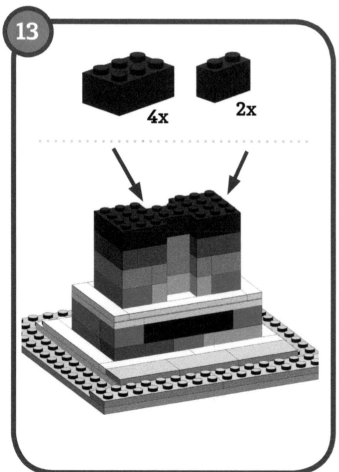

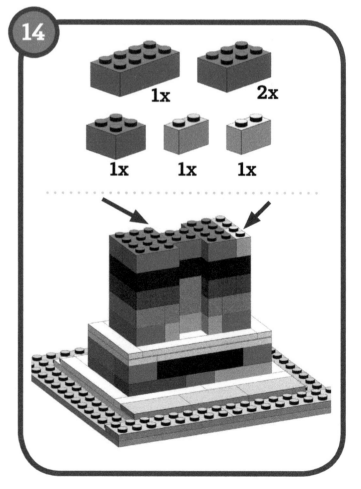

15

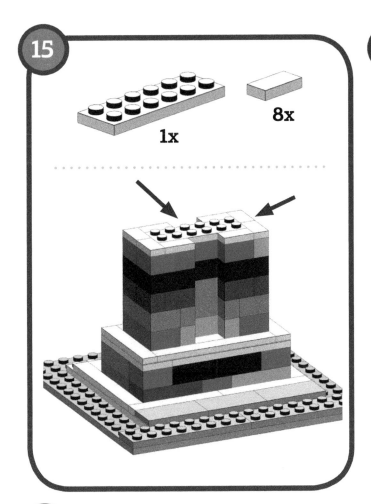

1x   8x

16

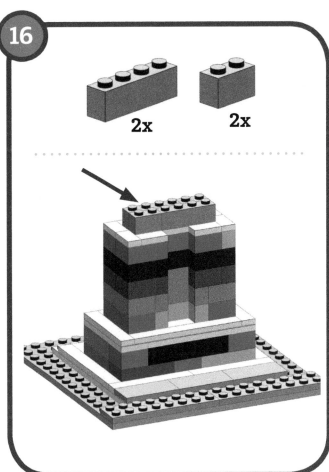

2x   2x

17

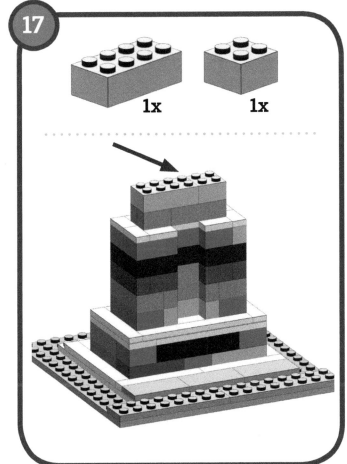

1x   1x

18

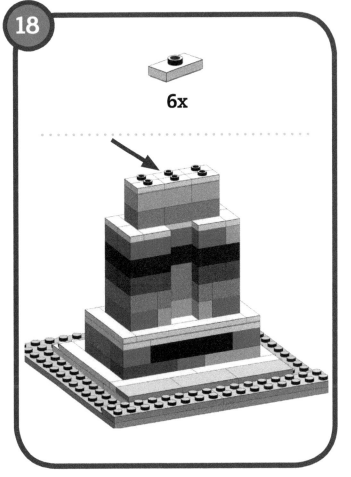

6x

19

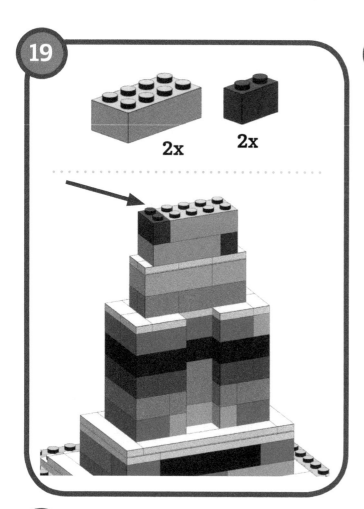

2x   2x

20

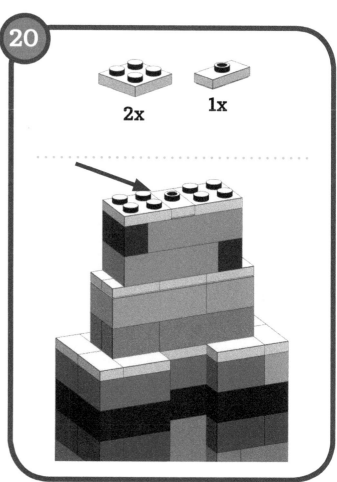

2x   1x

21

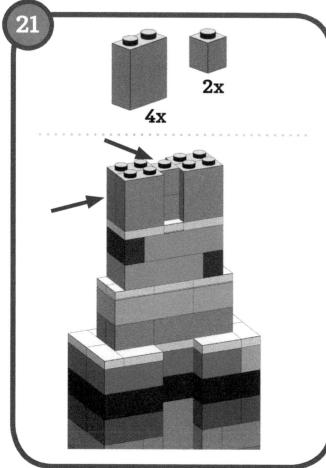

4x   2x

22

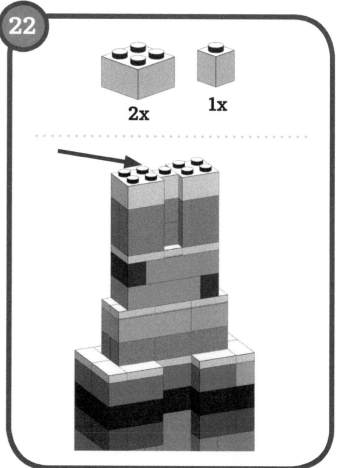

2x   1x

16

23

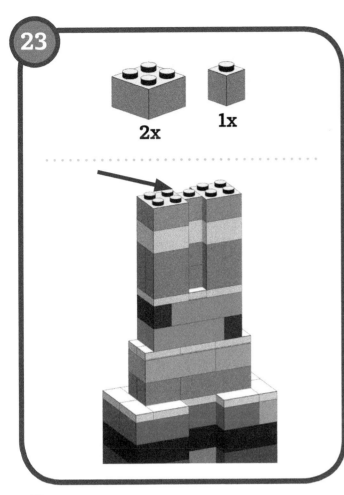

2x   1x

24

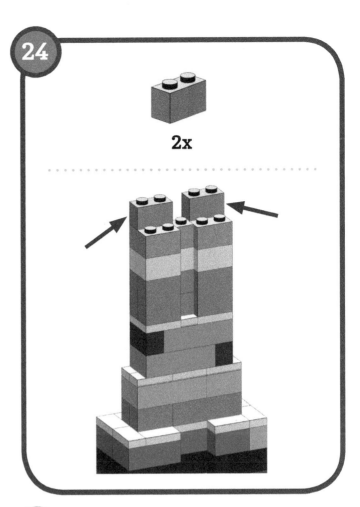

2x

25

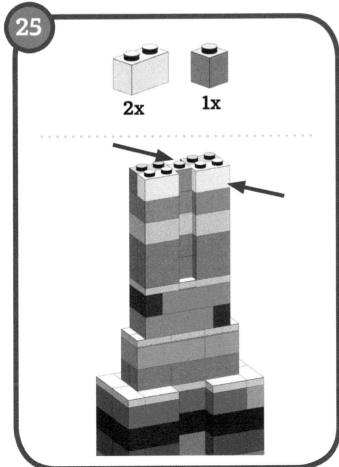

2x   1x

26

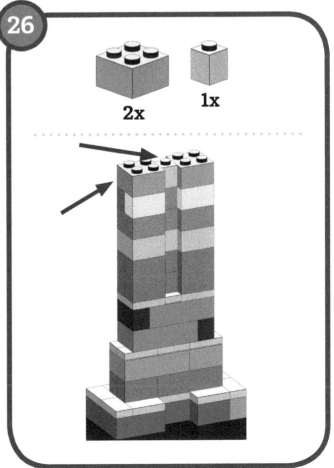

2x   1x

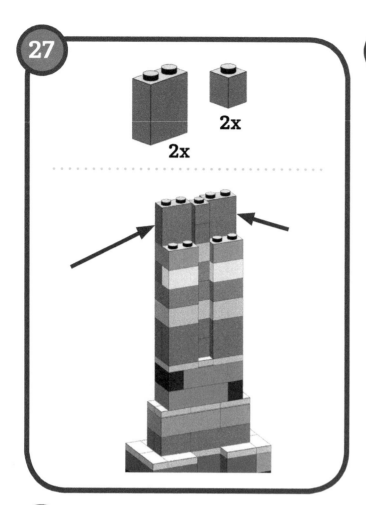

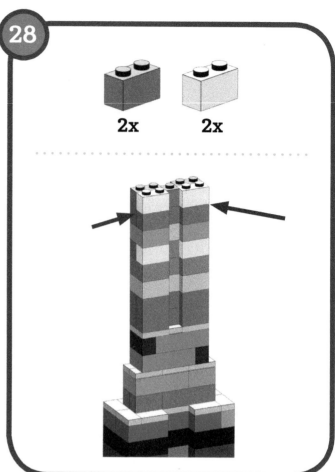

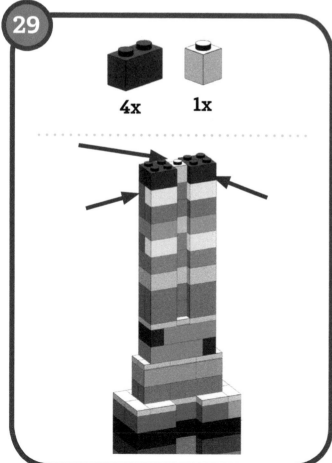

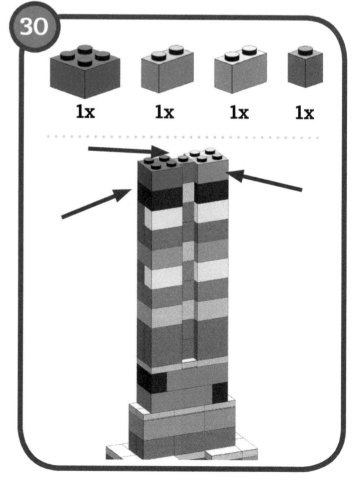

31

1x   1x   2x   1x

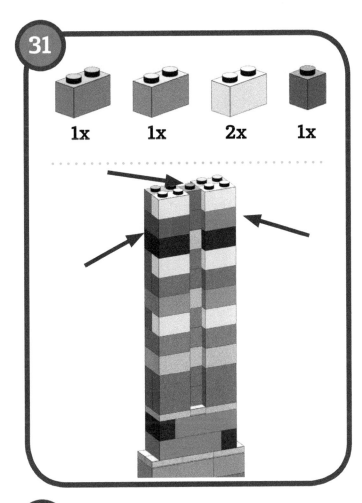

32

2x   1x

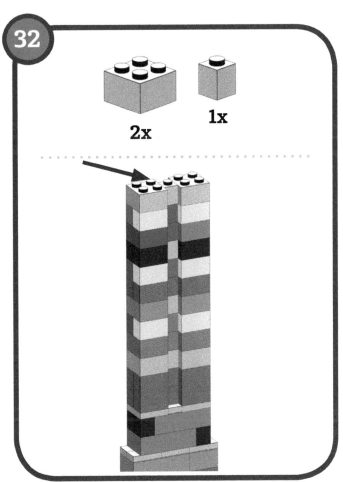

33

1x   4x   1x

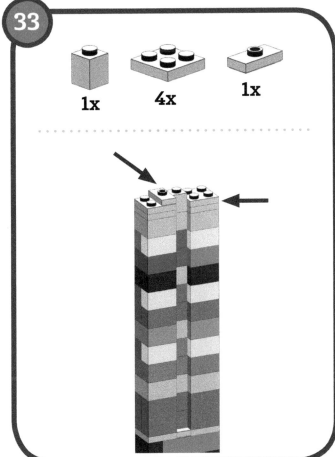

34

2x   1x

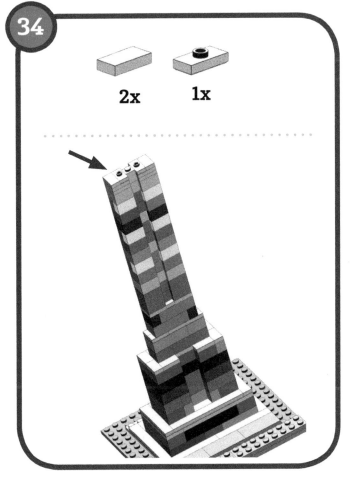

35

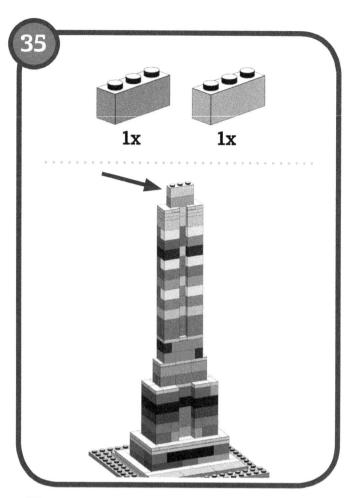

1x 1x

36

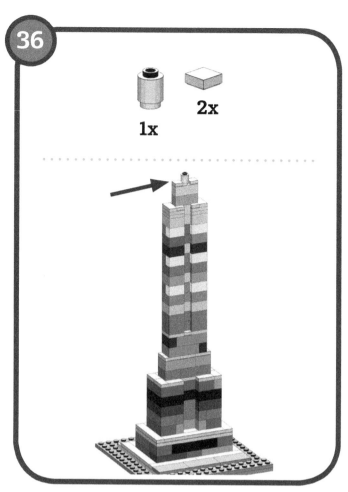

1x 2x

37

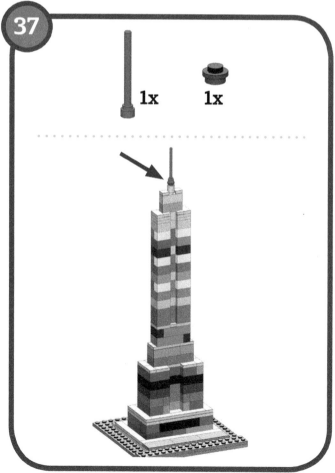

1x 1x

The Eiffel Tower

Build the Eiffel Tower

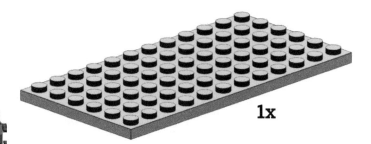

1x

5x

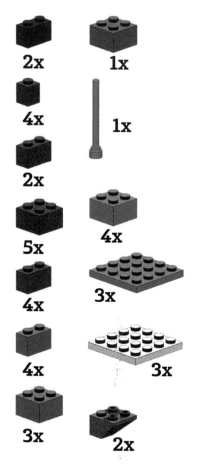

2x

1x

4x

1x

2x

5x

4x

4x

3x

4x

3x

3x

2x

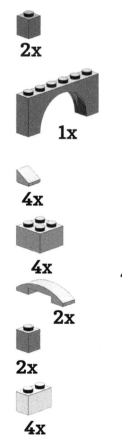

2x

1x

4x

4x

2x

2x

4x

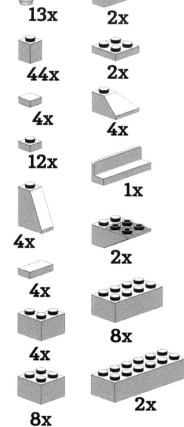

13x

44x

4x

12x

4x

4x

2x

8x

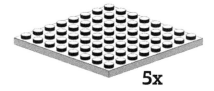

2x

2x

4x

1x

2x

8x

2x

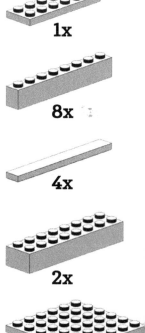

1x

8x

4x

2x

1x

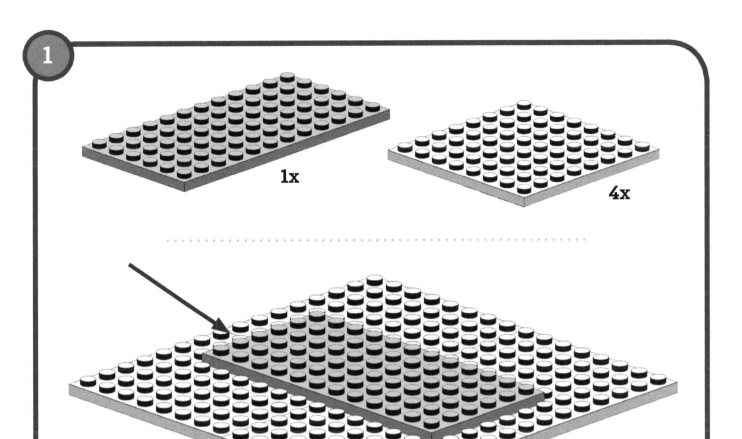

1x

4x

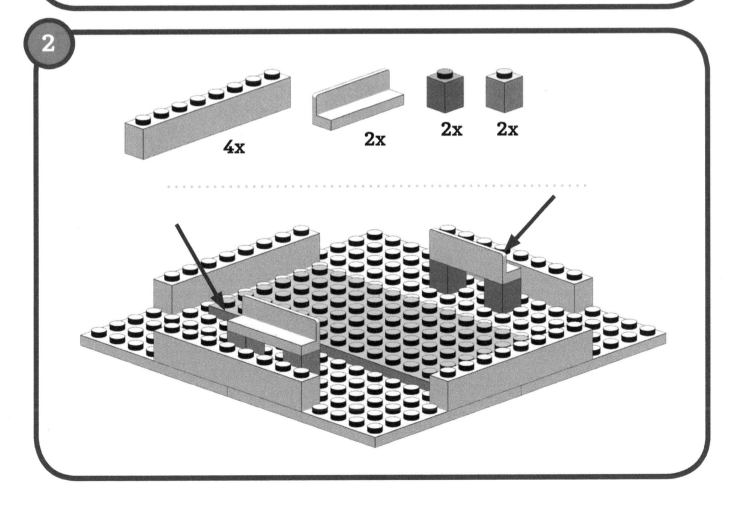

4x

2x

2x

2x

4x

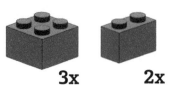

3x   2x

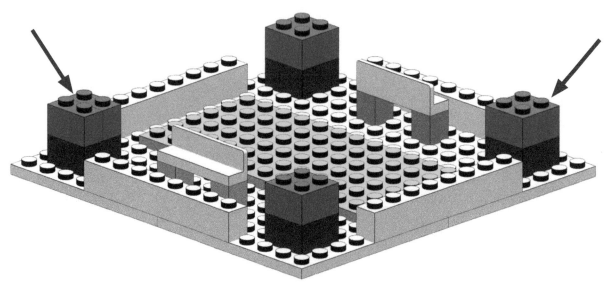

5

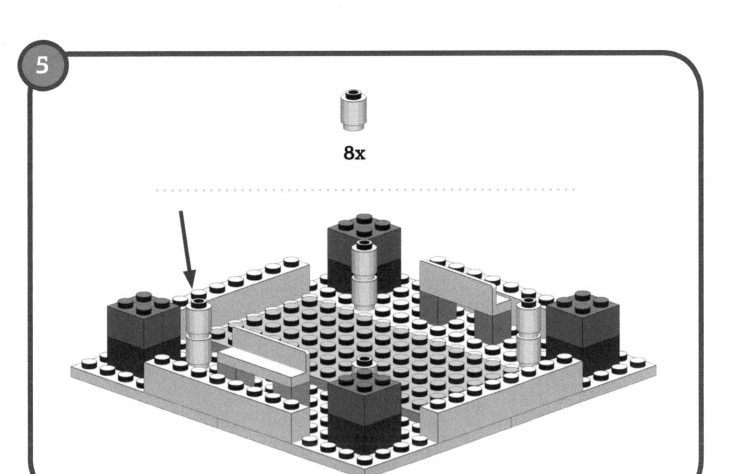

8x

6

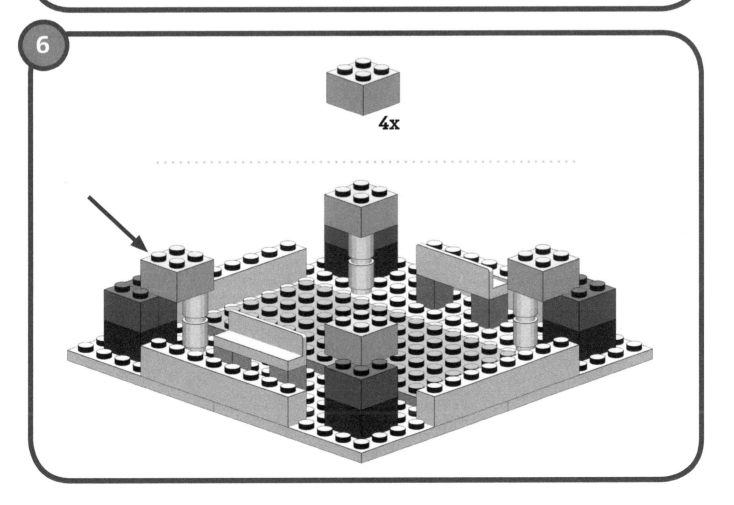

4x

8x

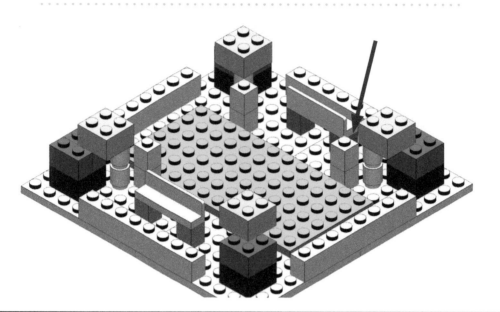

4x

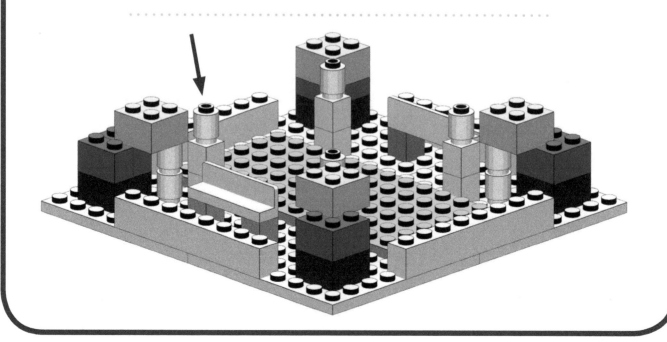

4x

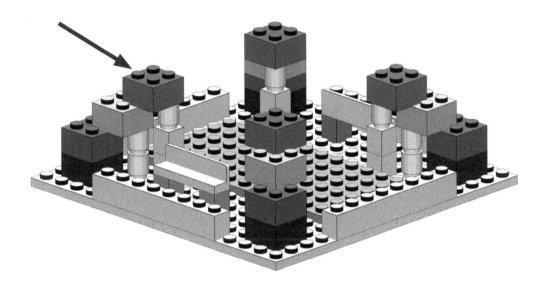

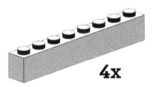 4x 4x

11

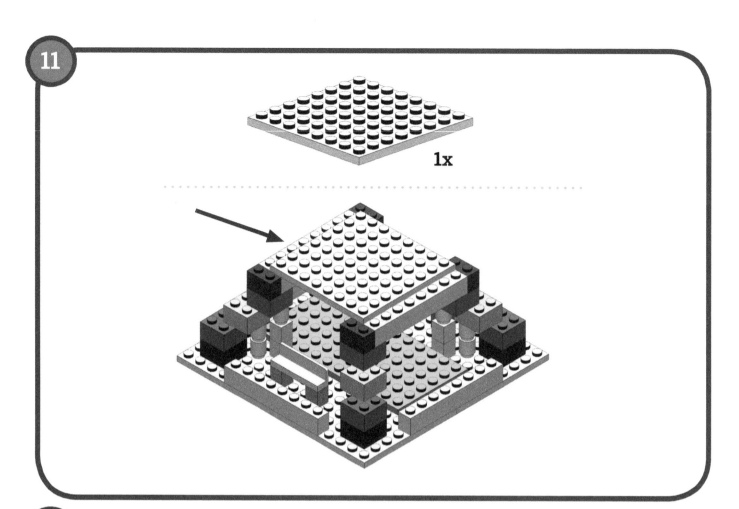

1x

12

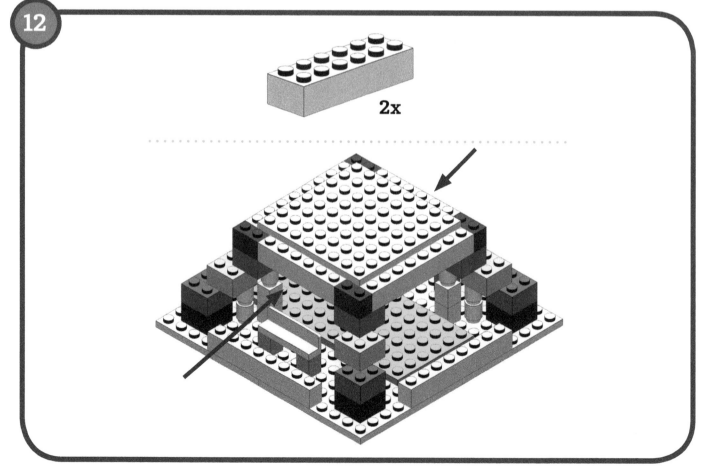

2x

28

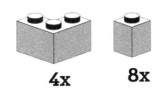

4x   8x

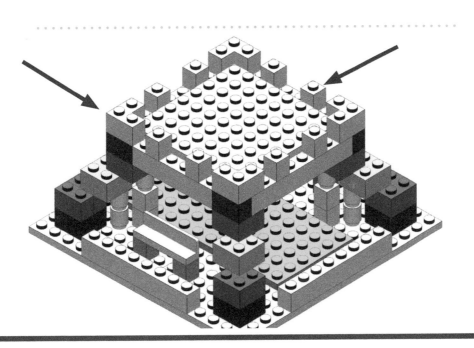

4x   4x

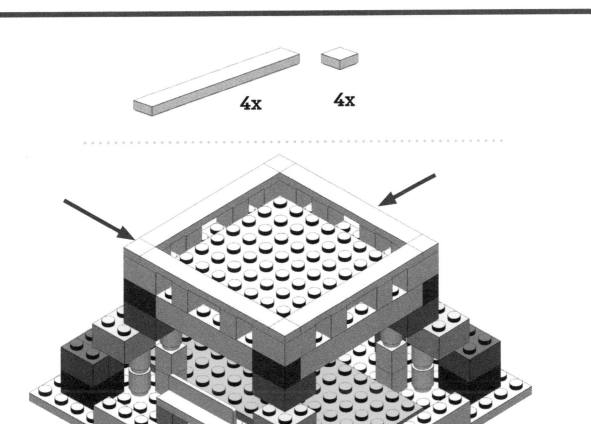

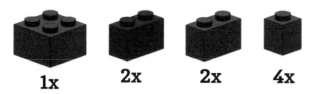

1x   2x   2x   4x

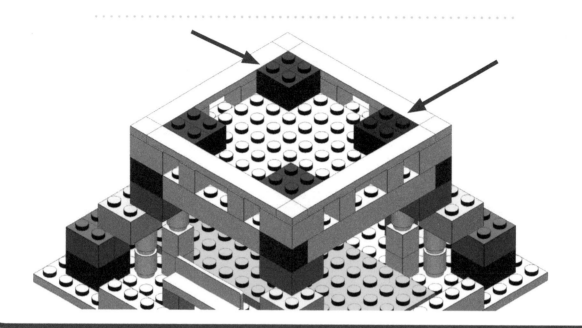

16

4x

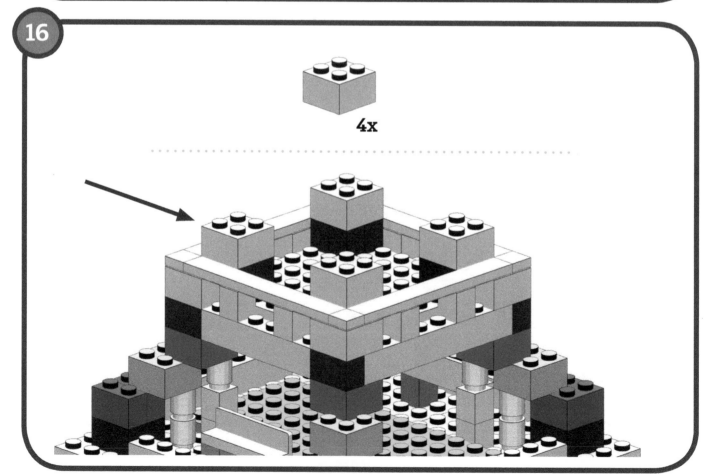

17

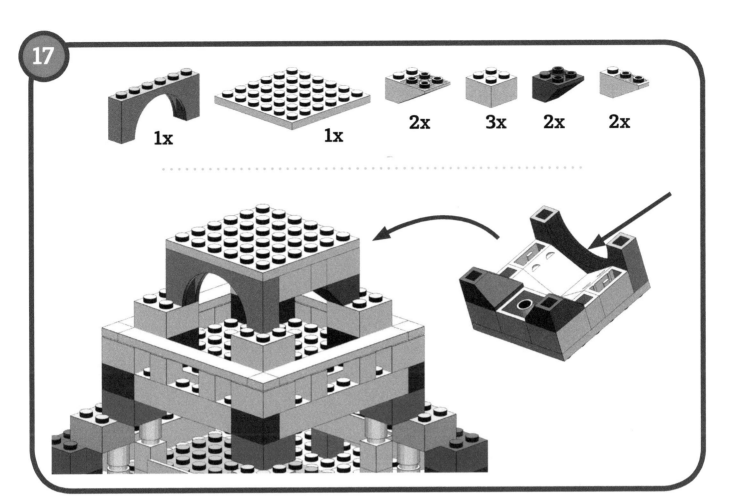

1x 1x 2x 3x 2x 2x

18

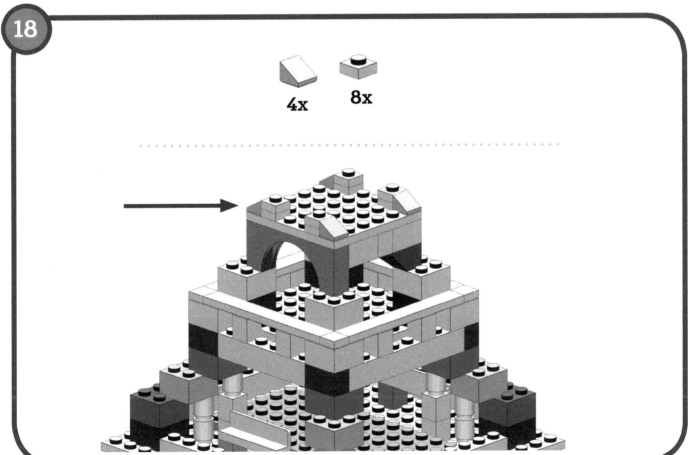

4x 8x

2x

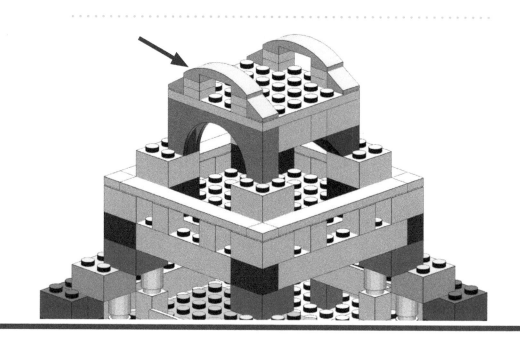

4x

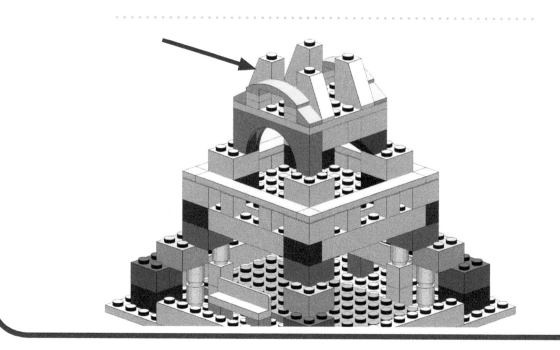

21

1x

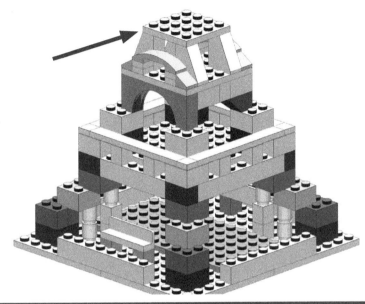

22

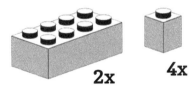

2x   4x

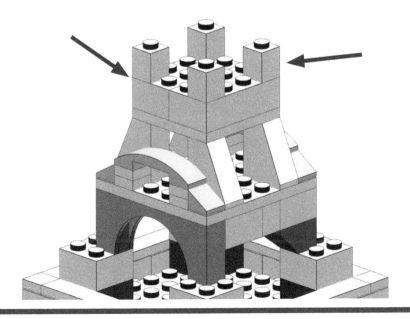

33

23

1x 4x

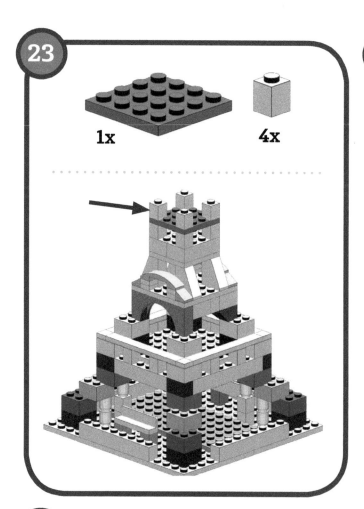

24

2x 4x

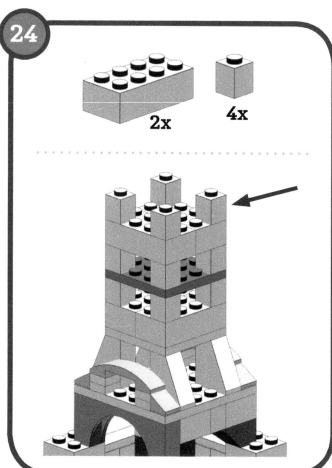

25

1x 4x

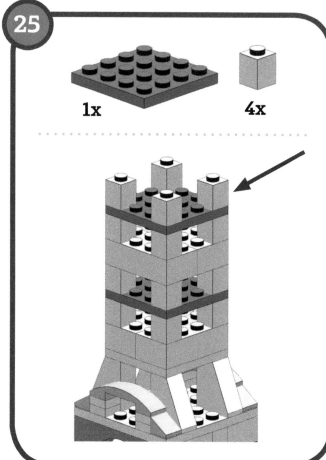

26

2x

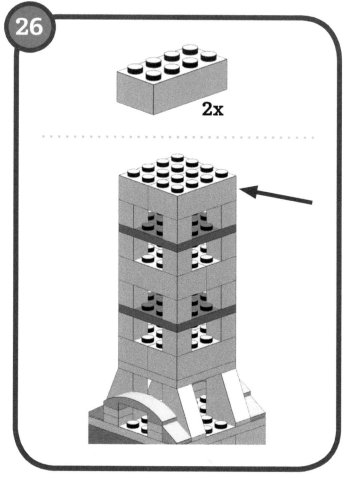

27

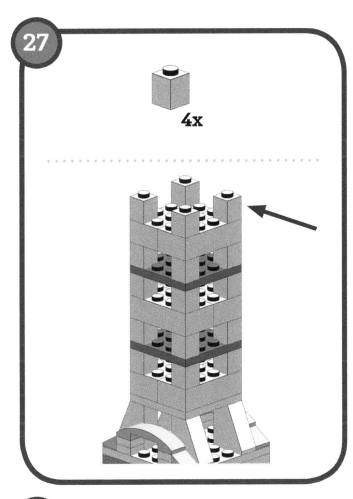

4x

28

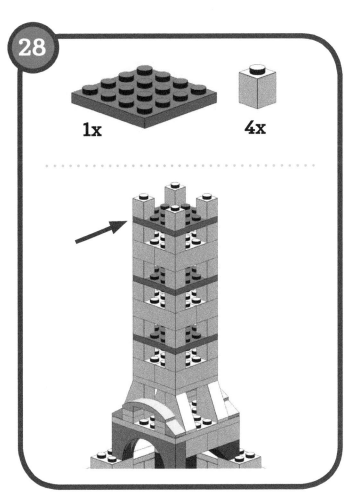

1x   4x

29

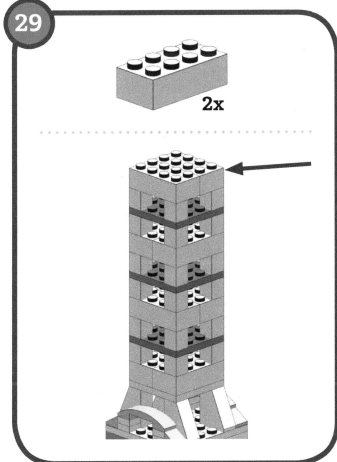

2x

30

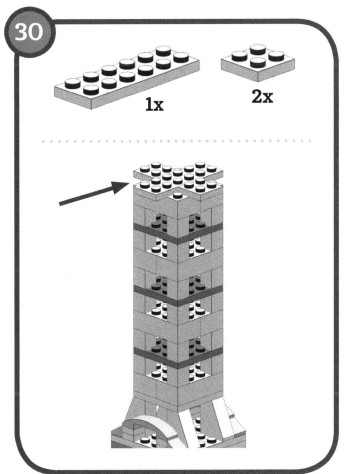

1x   2x

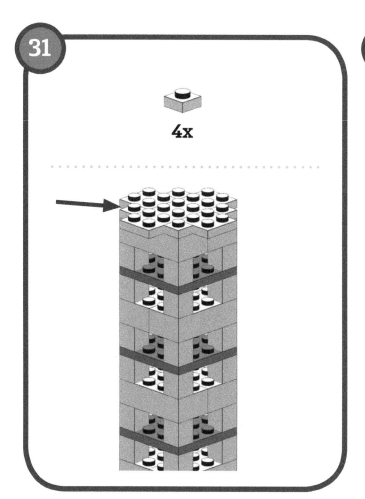

4x

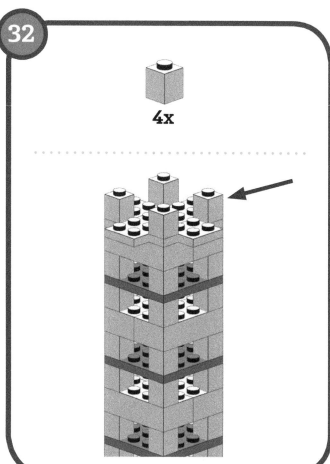

4x

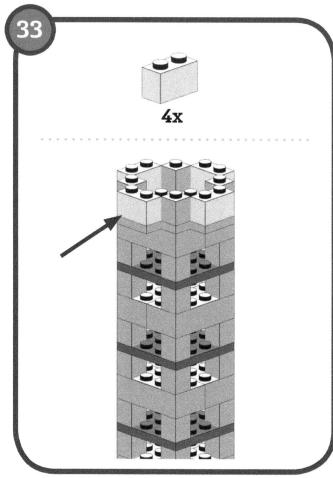

4x

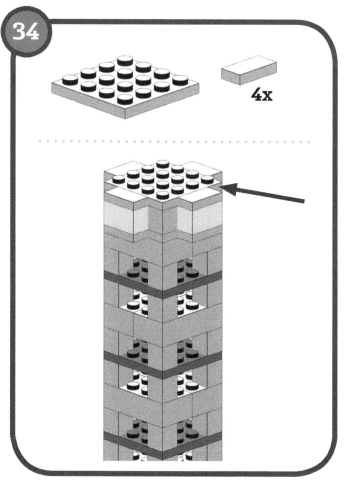

4x

35

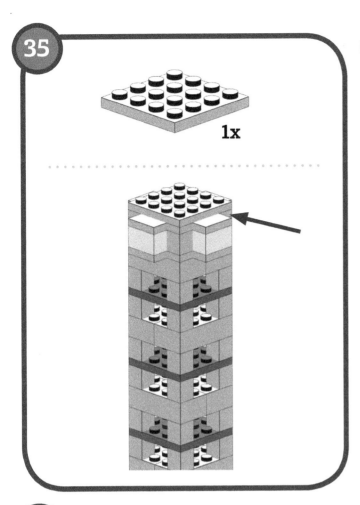

1x

36

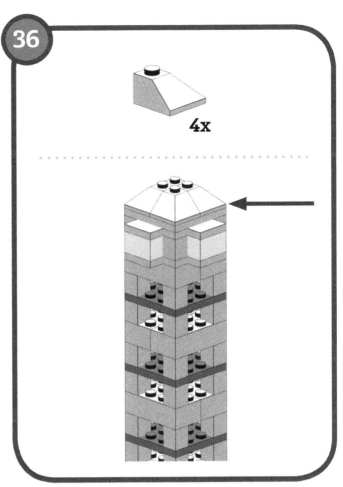

4x

37

1x 1x 1x 1x

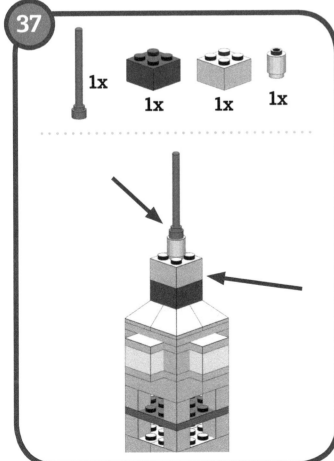

Taj Mahal

Build the Taj Mahal

1x

1x

1x

8x

8x

8x

3x

2x

2x

2x

11x

4x

11x

4x

2x

2x

23x

8x

17x

9x

8x

3x

21x

8x

21x

7x

8x

30x

4x

8x

1x

4x

35x

4x

8x

8x

10x

3x

10x

16x

12x

20x

11x

16x

12x

2x

10x

9x

10x

12x

11x

4x

40

1

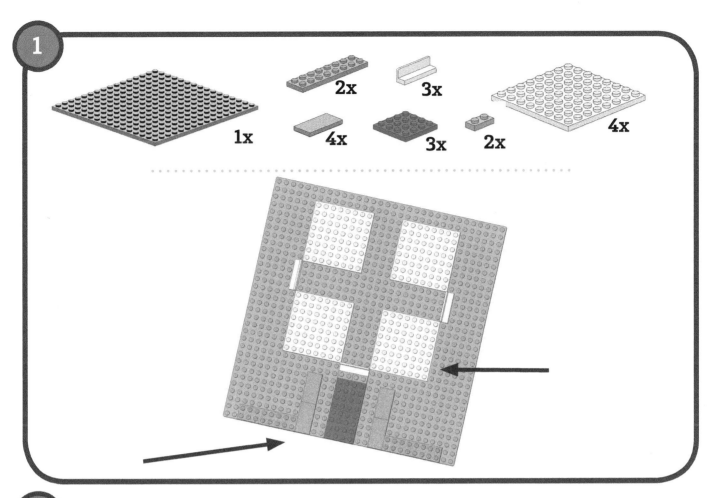

1x 2x 3x 4x 3x 2x 4x

2

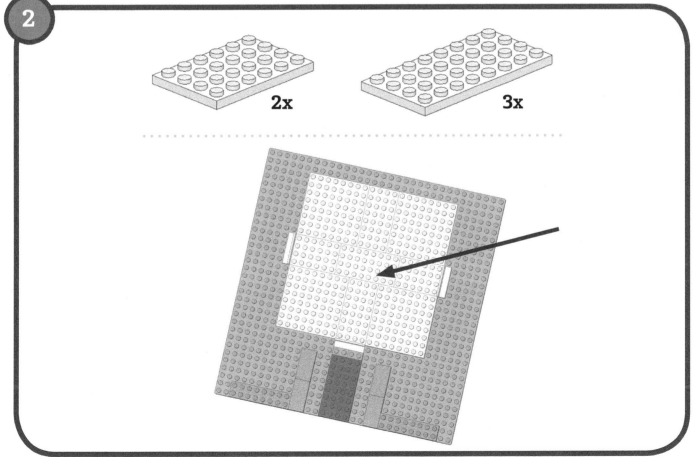

2x 3x

3

16x

13x

3x

8x

3x

5x

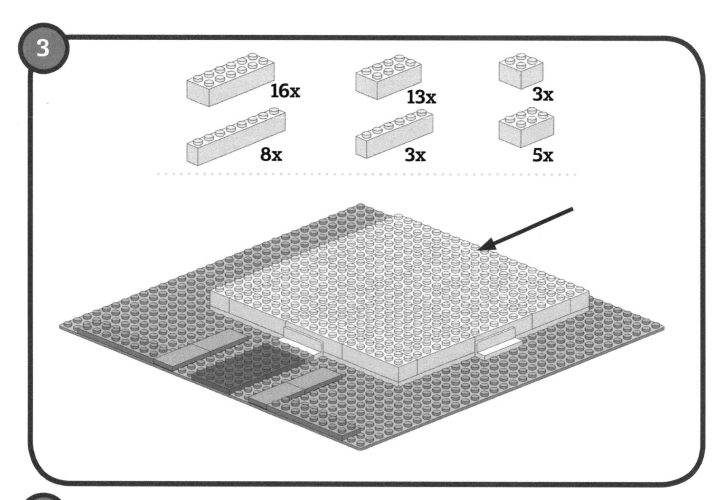

4

20x

2x

11x

6x

7x

2x

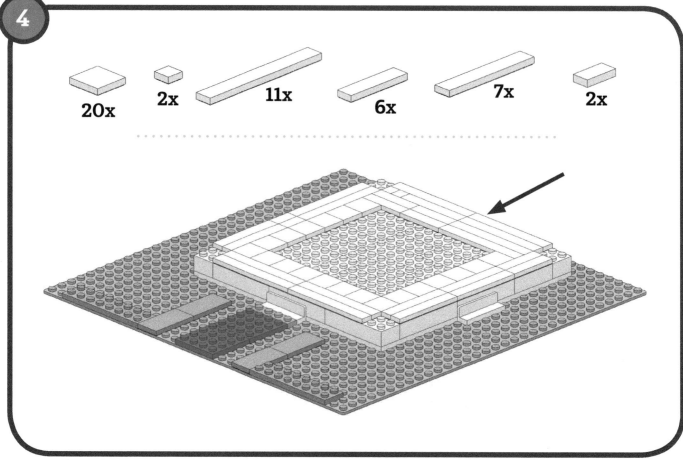

5

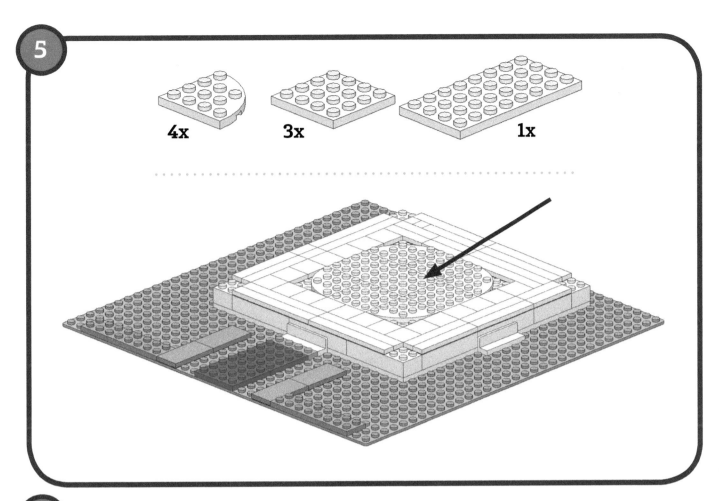

4x   **3x**   **1x**

6

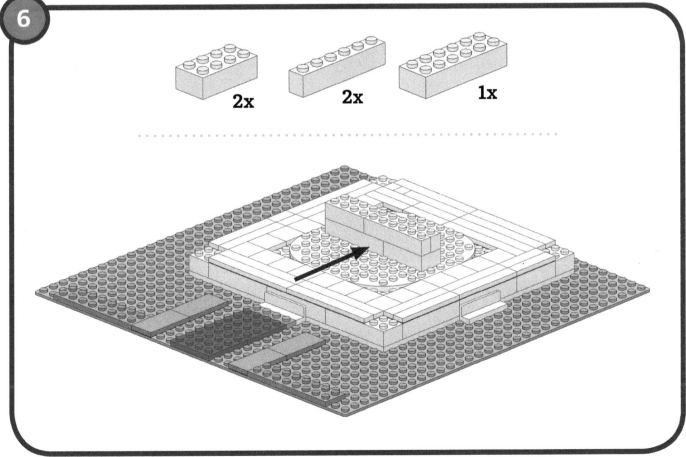

2x   **2x**   **1x**

7

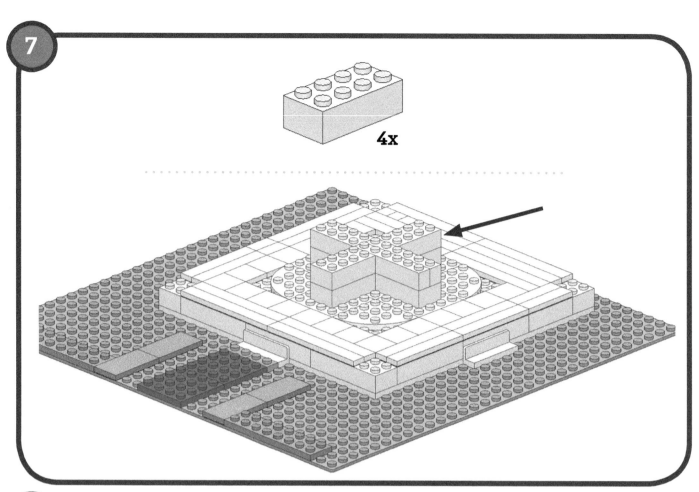

4x

8

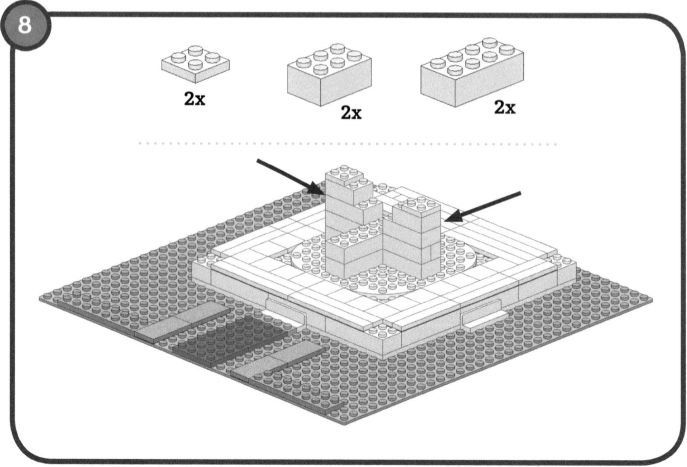

2x   2x   2x

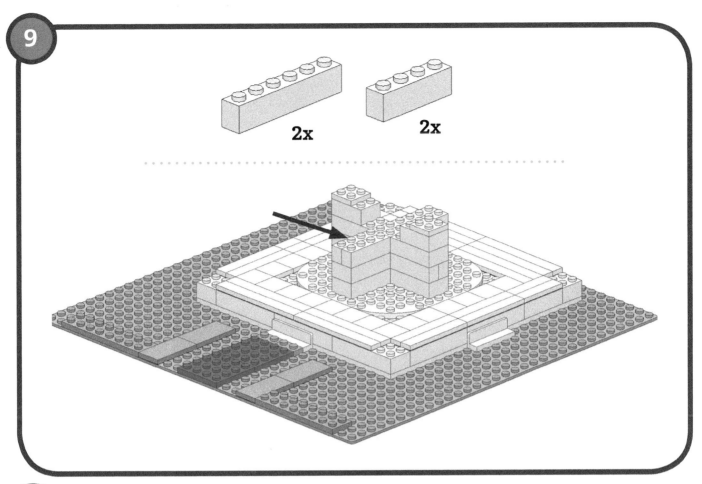

9

2x   2x

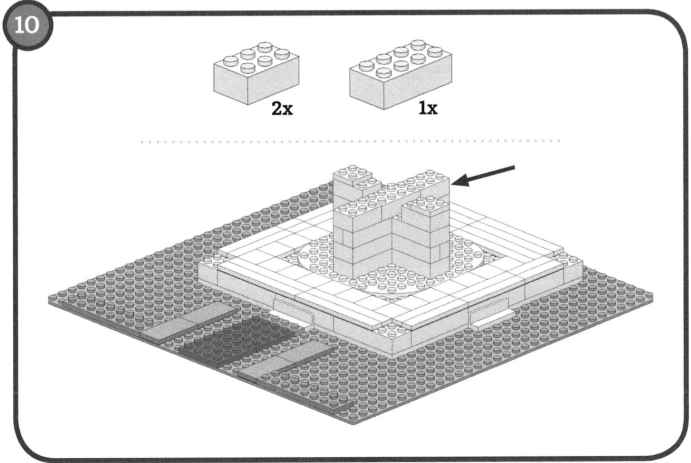

10

2x   1x

11

2x 1x 2x 7x 1x

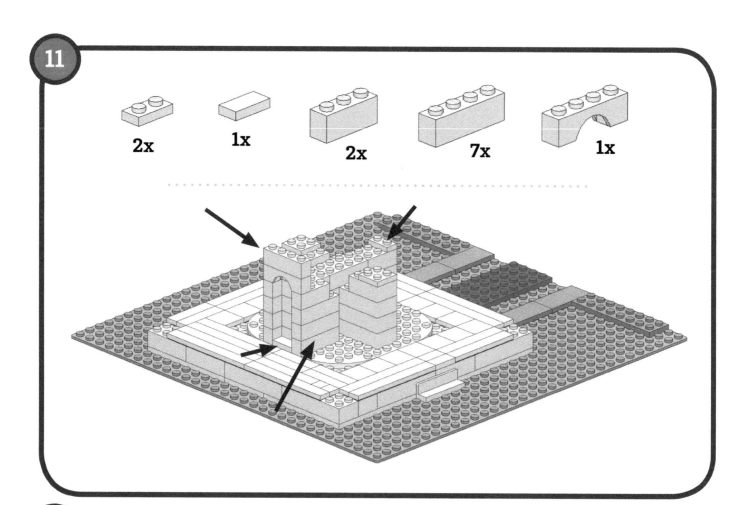

12

1x 2x 7x 1x

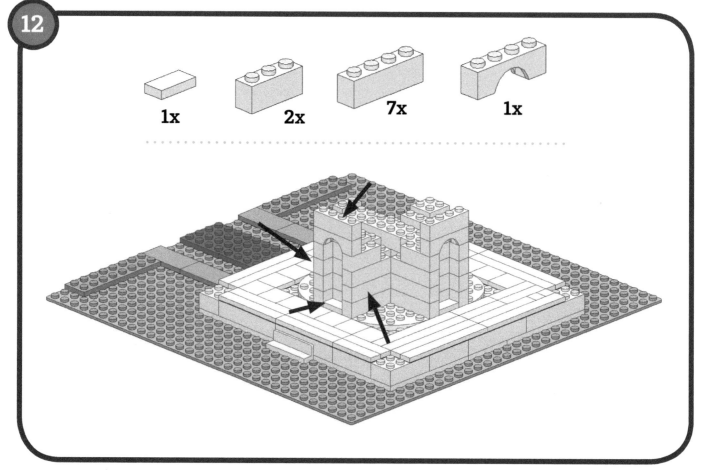

46

13

1x 2x 7x 1x

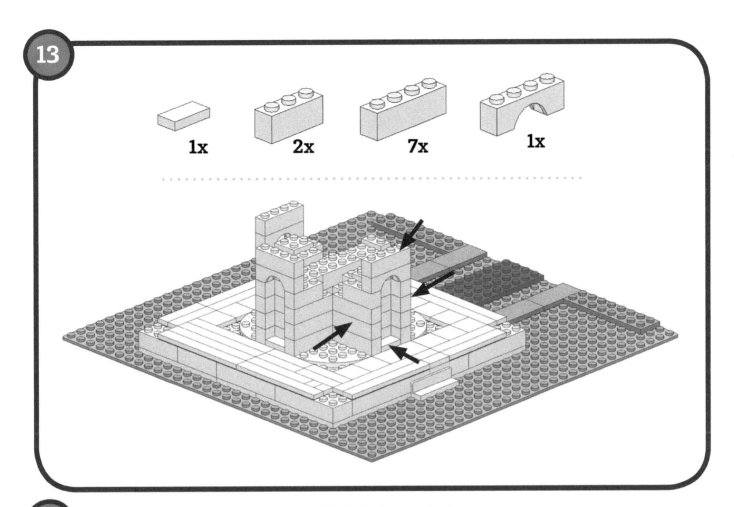

14

1x 2x 7x 1x

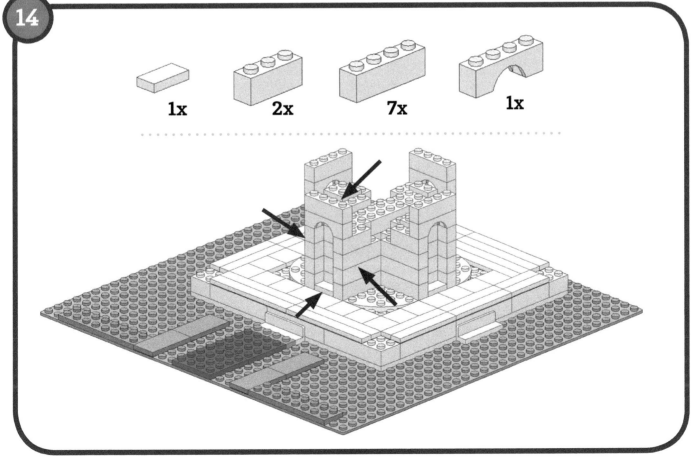

15

15x 4x 2x

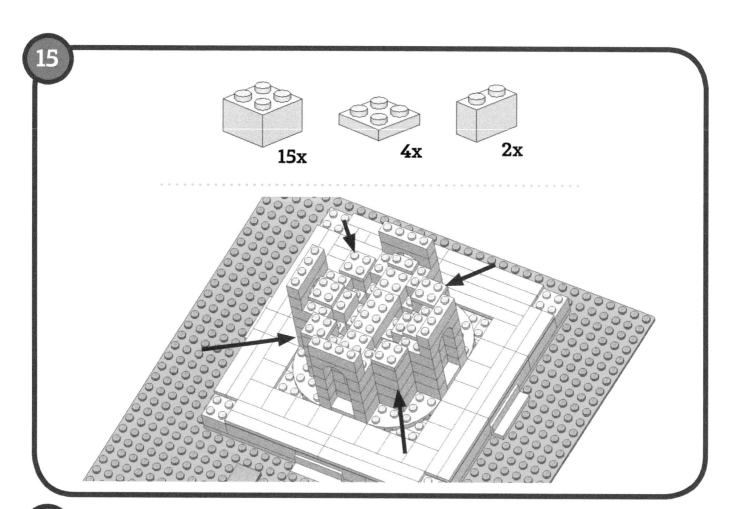

16

4x 2x

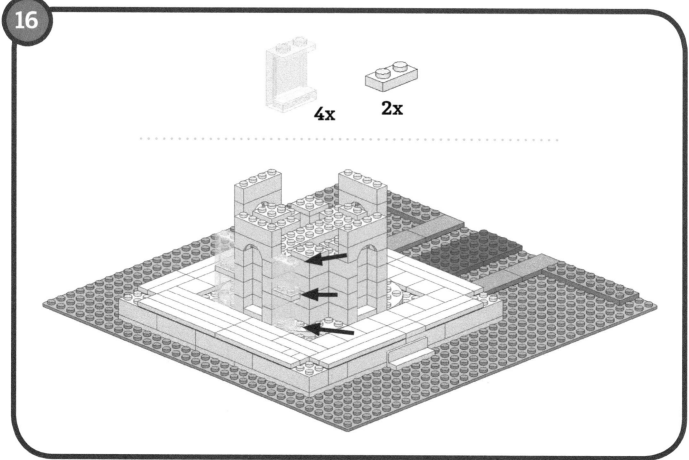

17

4x 2x

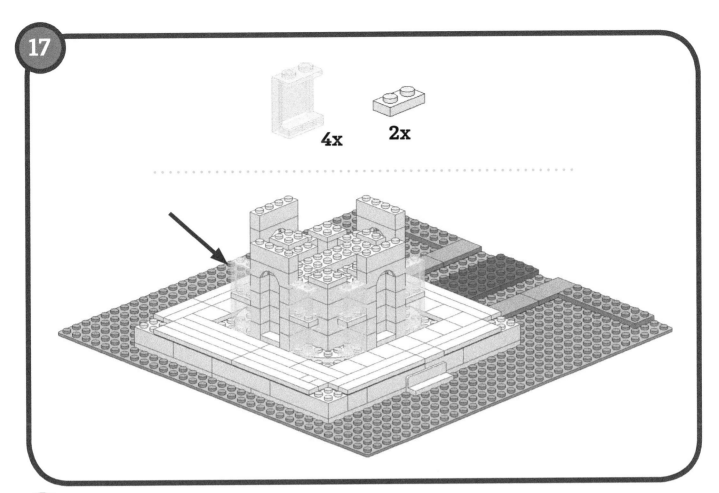

18

4x 2x

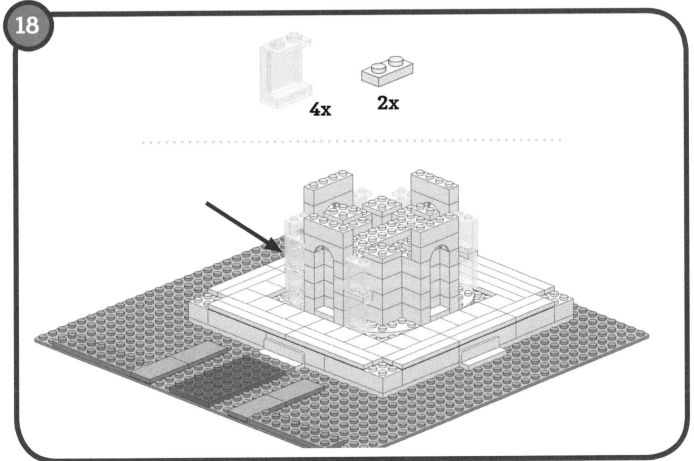

19

4x 2x

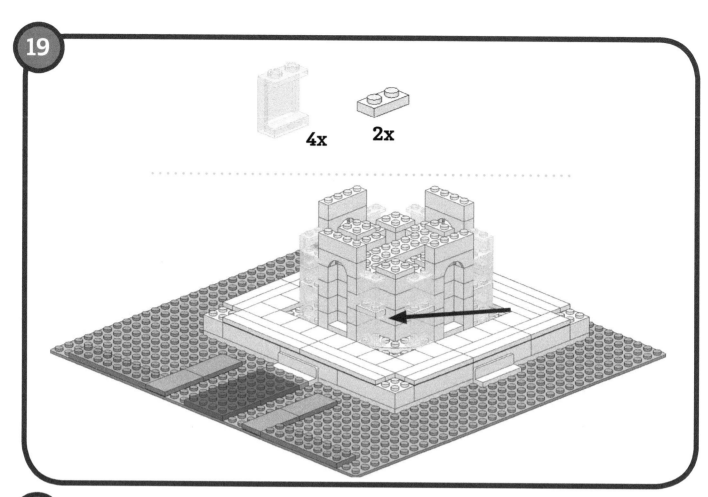

20

2x 6x 2x

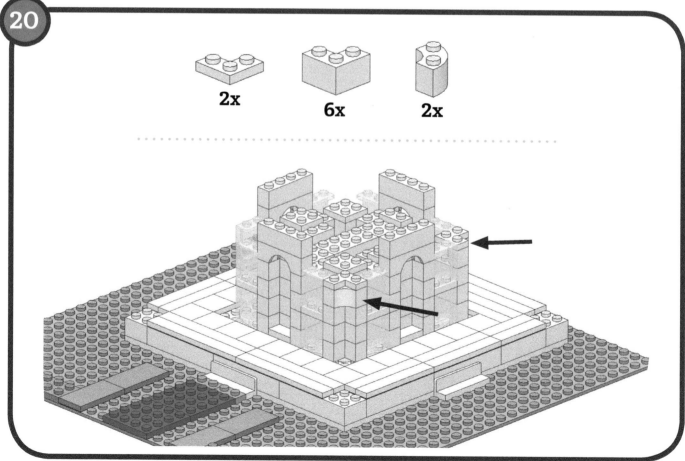

21

2x 6x 2x

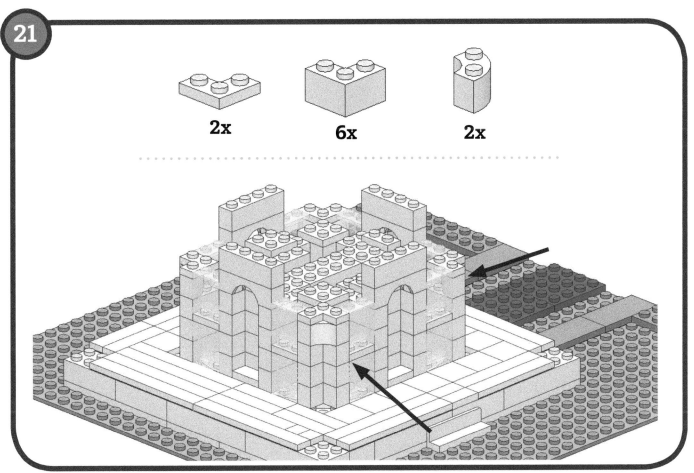

22

8x

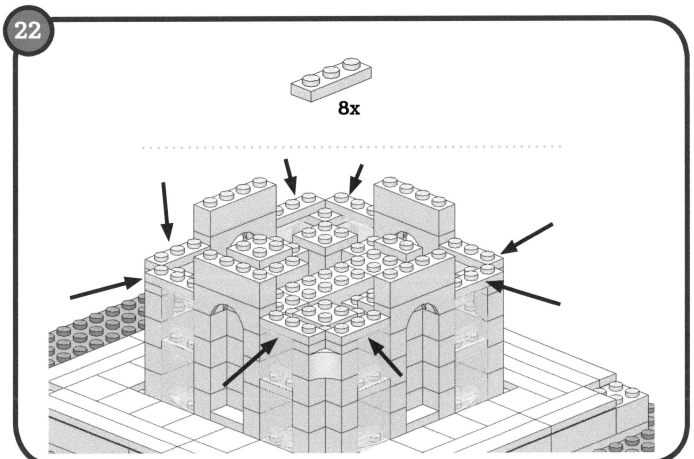

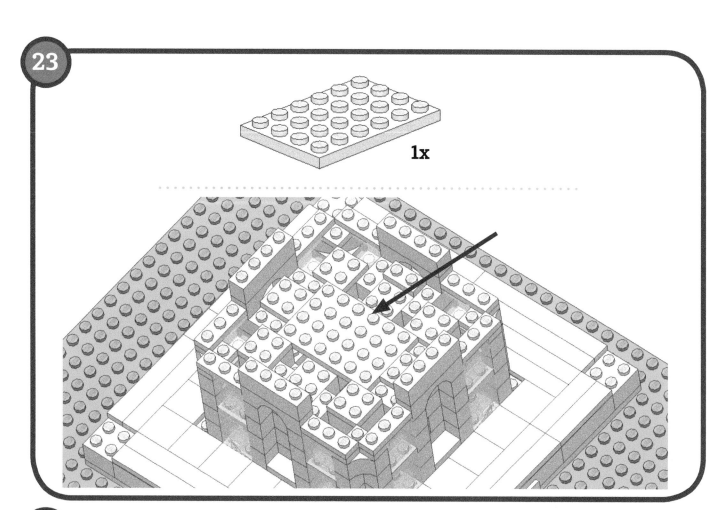

23

1x

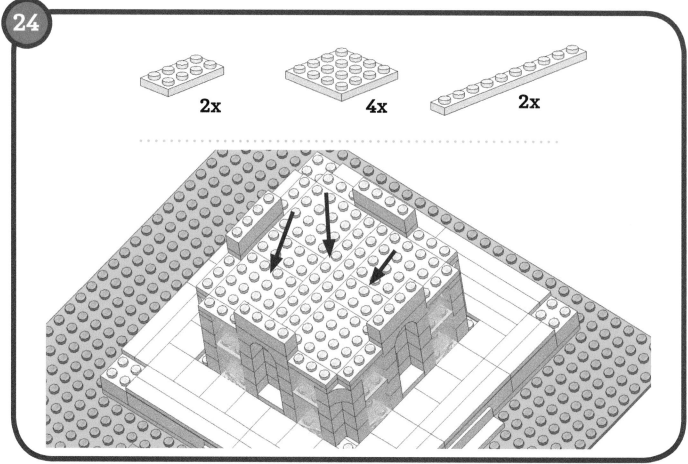

24

2x

4x

2x

25

1x **3x** **3x**

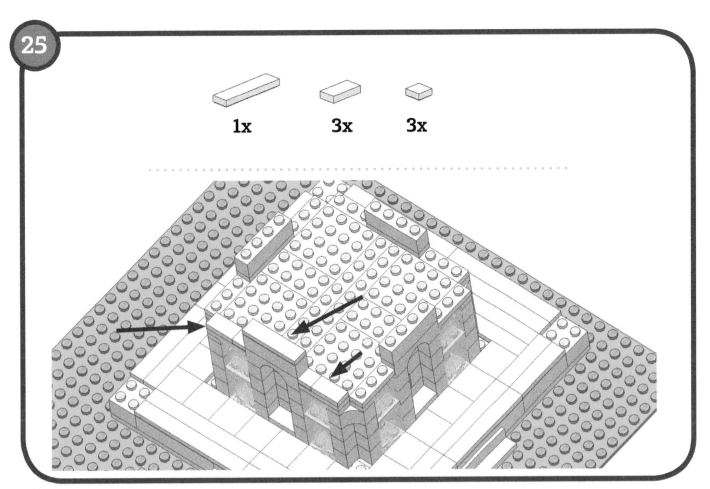

26

1x **10x** **6x**

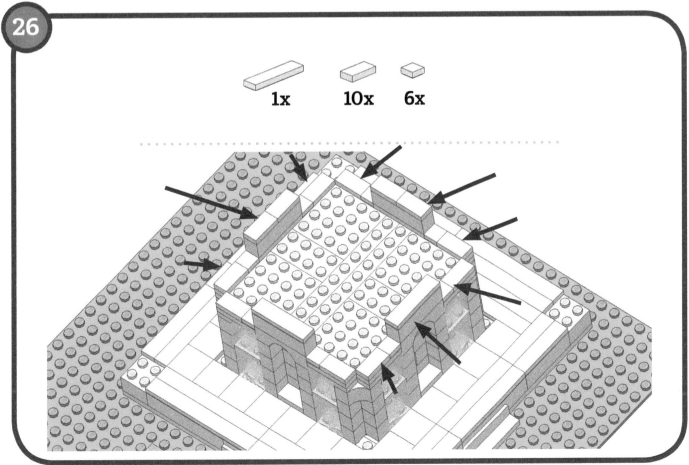

27

1x 2x

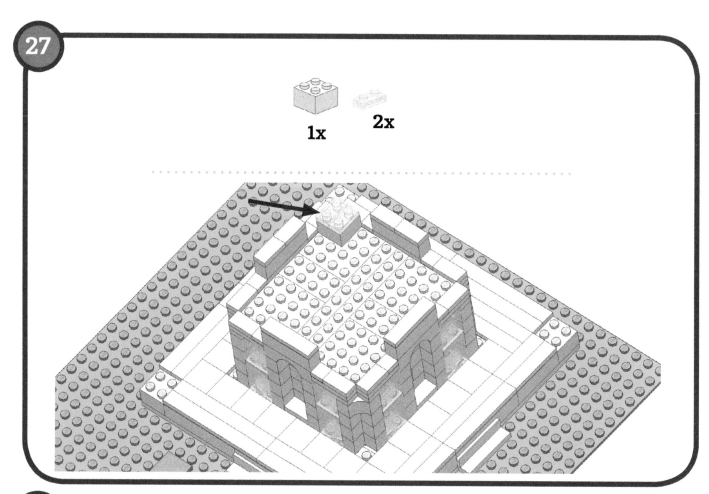

28

1x 1x 1x

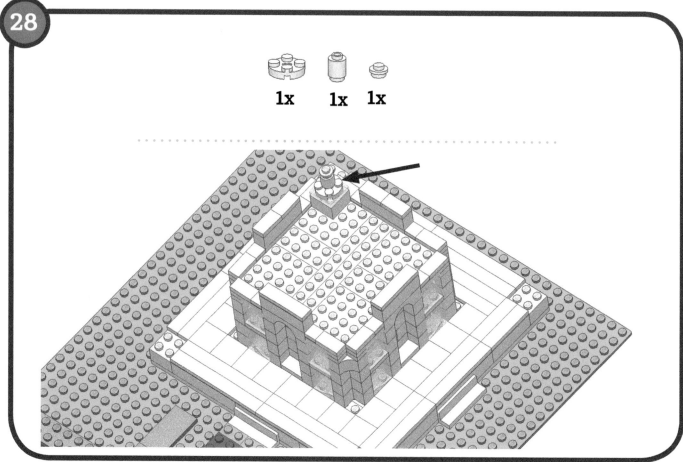

29

3x 3x 3x 6x 3x

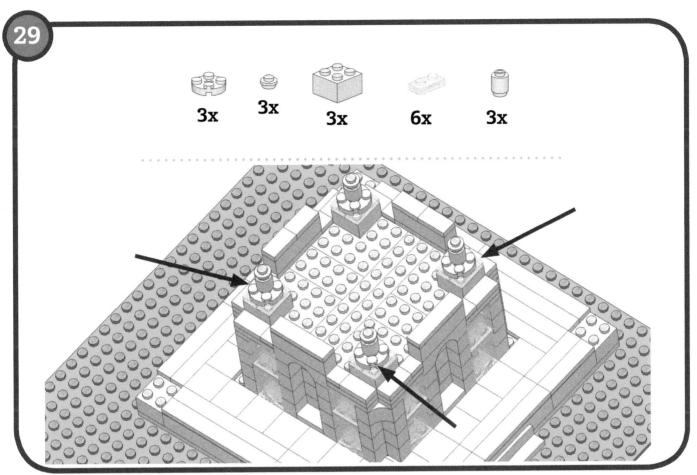

30

4x 4x

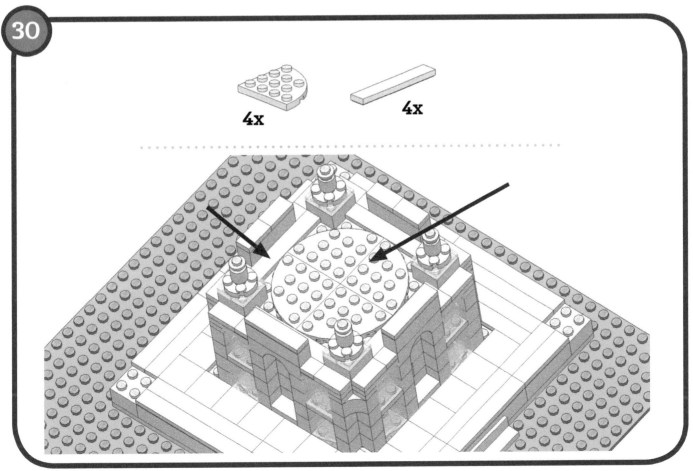

31

8x

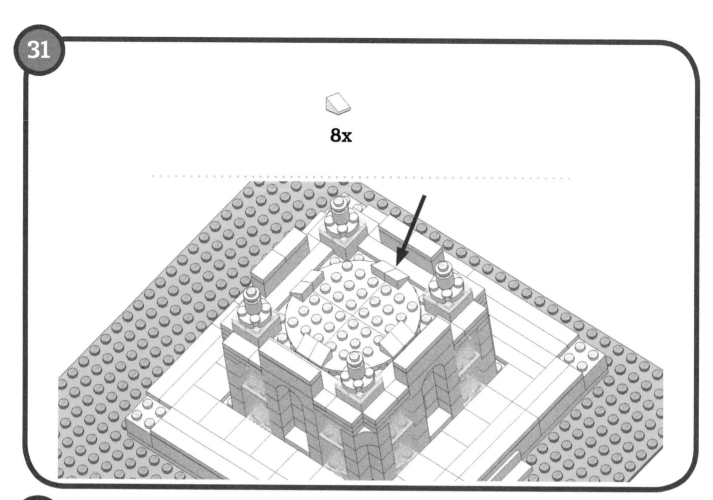

32

1x 5x 2x 1x

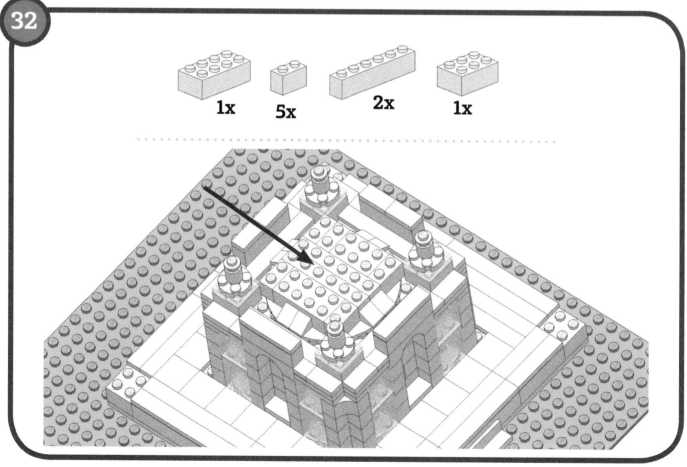

33

8x

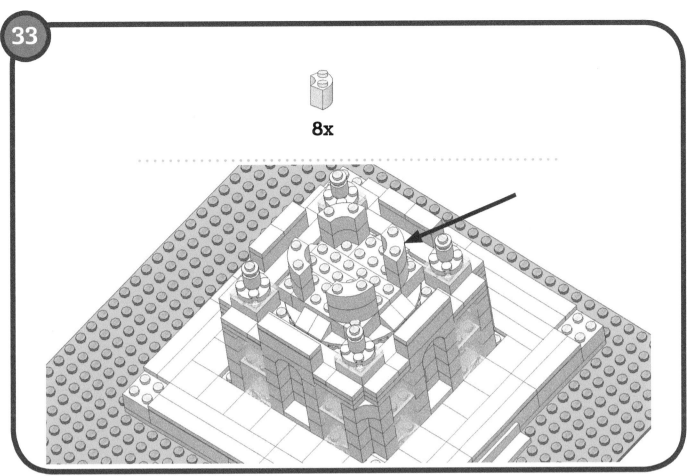

34

8x

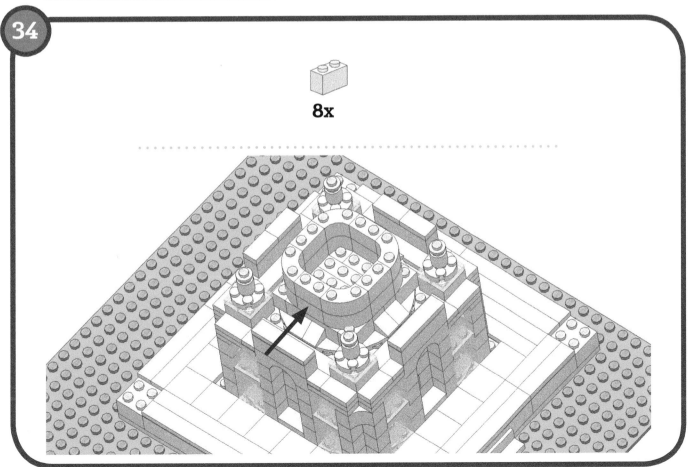

35

8x

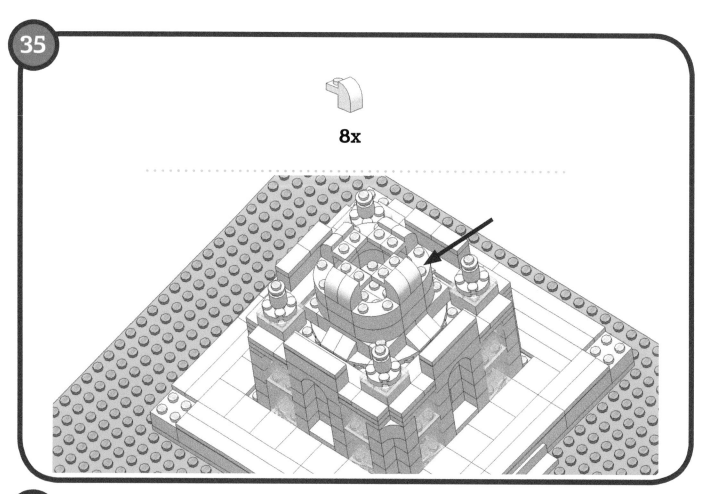

36

2x

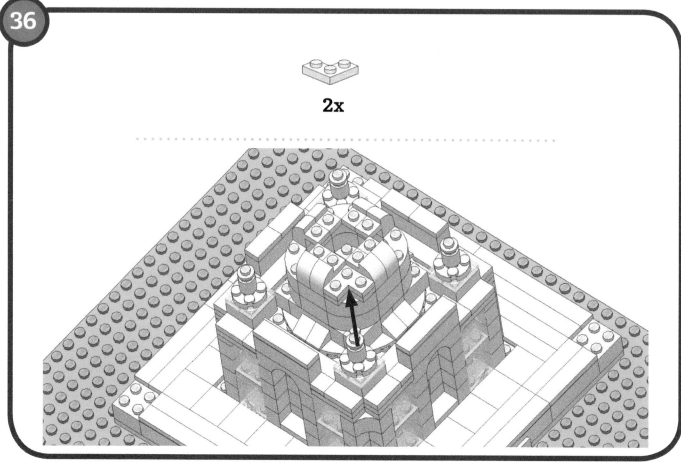

37

2x

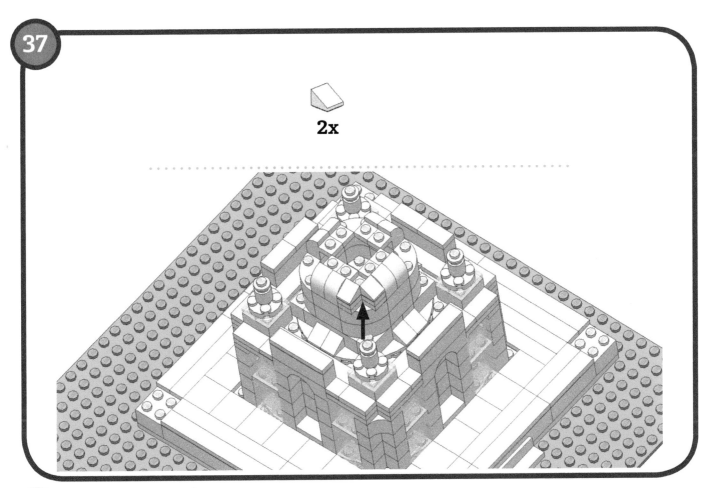

38

6x   **6x**

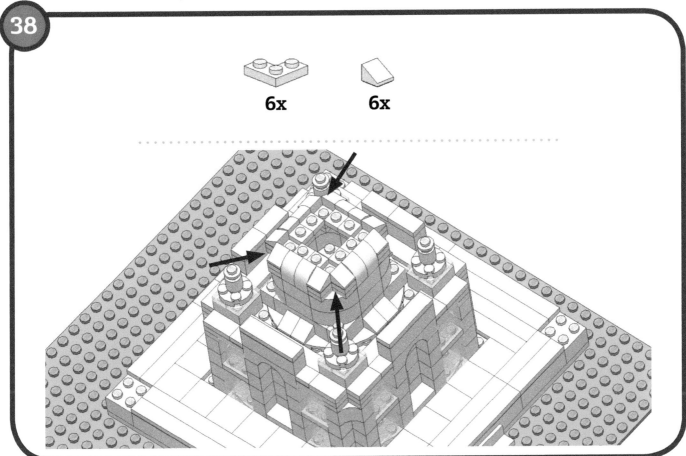

39

4x

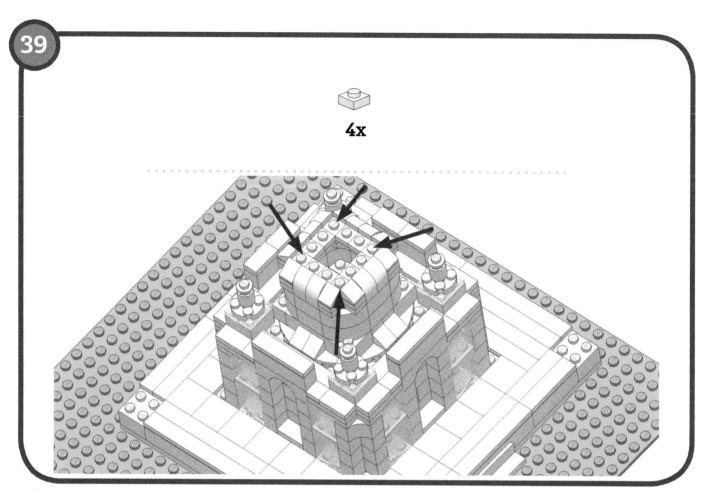

40

1x

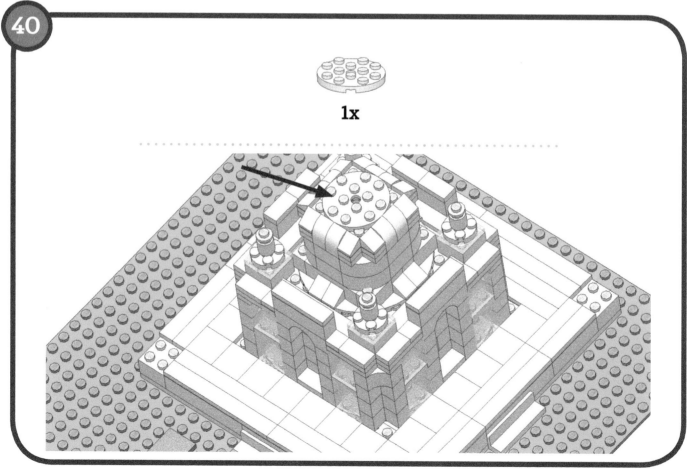

41

2x 2x

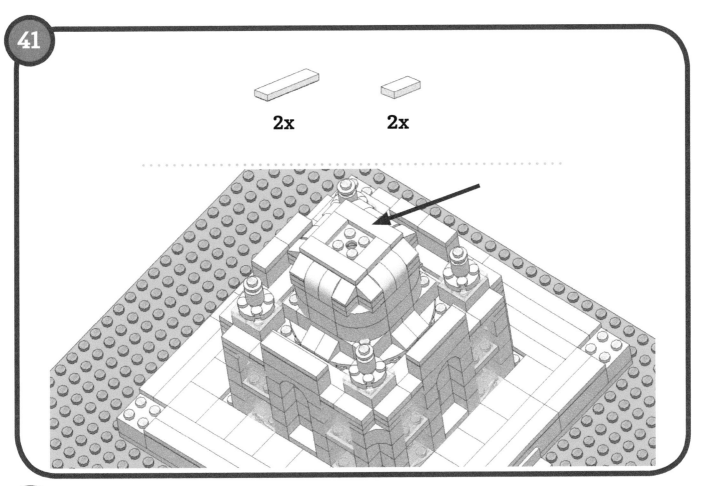

42

1x

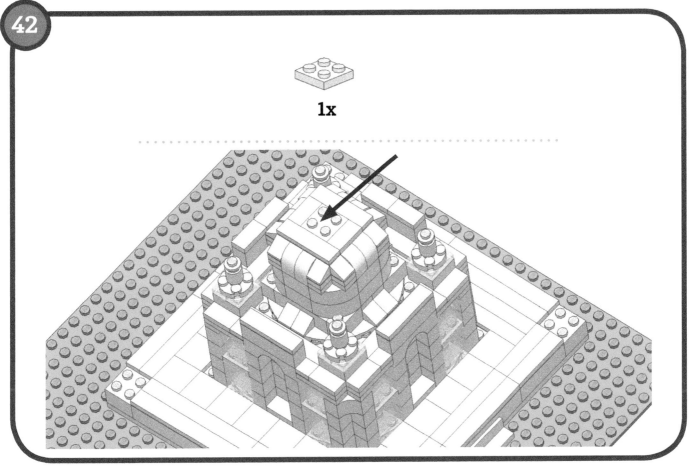

43

1x 2x

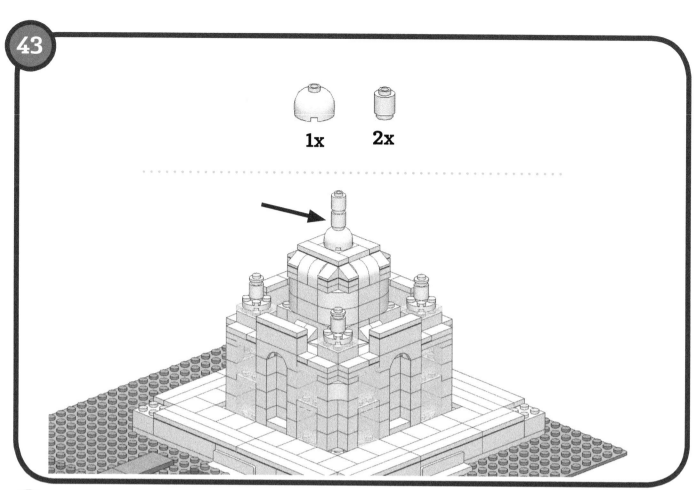

44

1x

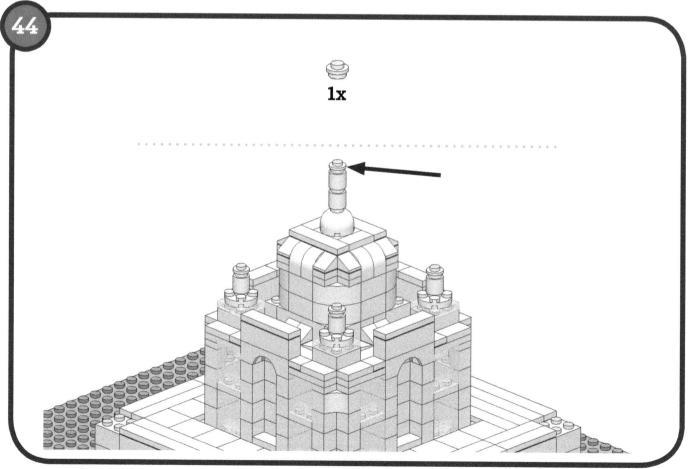

45

4x 2x

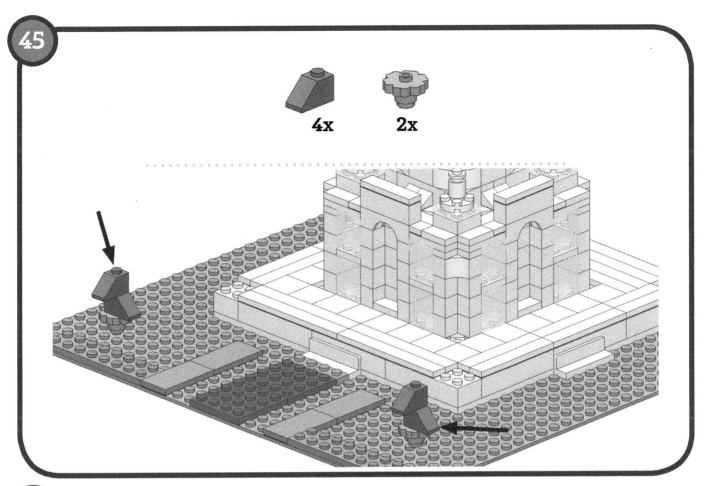

46

3x 2x

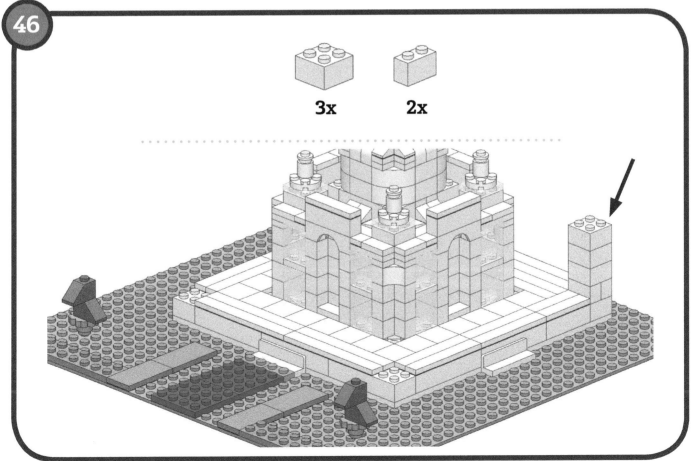

47

1x   3x

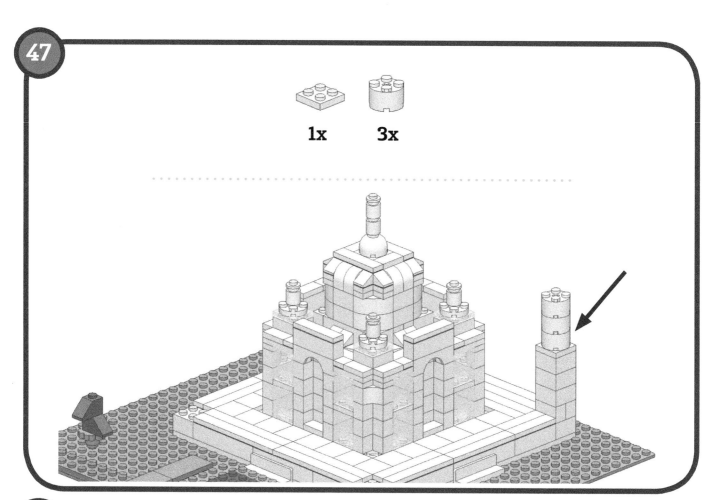

48

2x

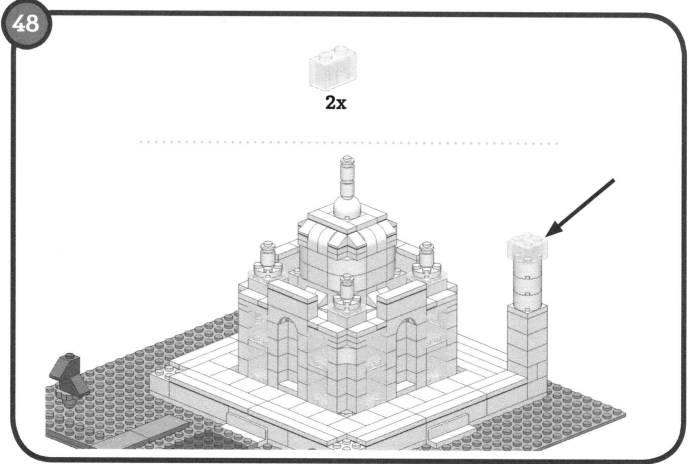

1x 1x 1x

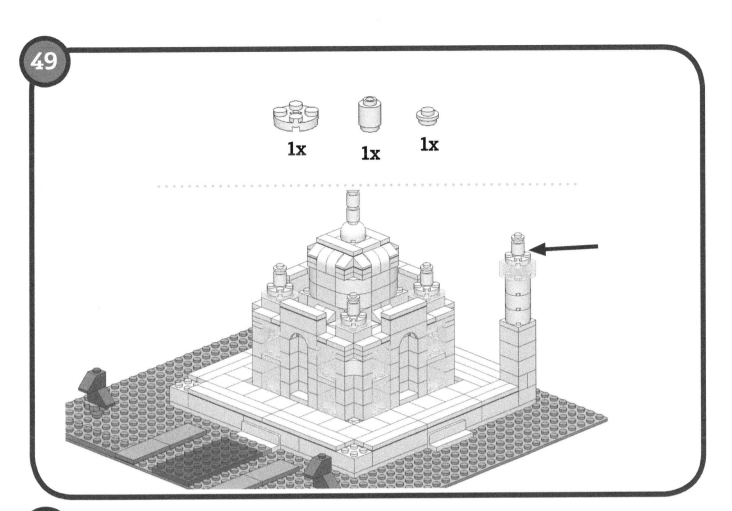

1x 2x 1x 1x 3x 2x 3x 1x

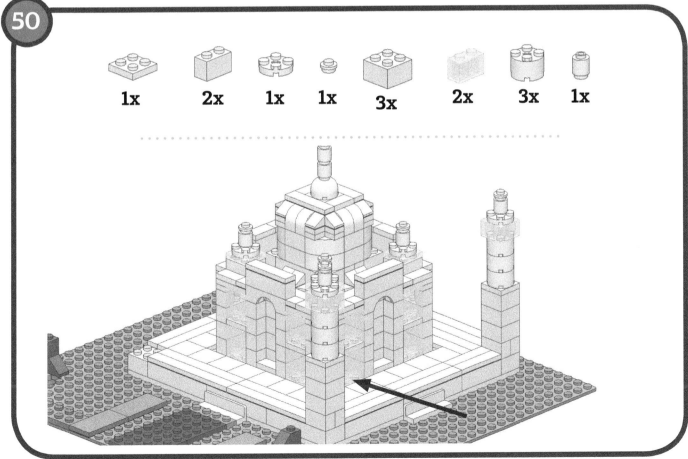

51

4x **1x** **2x** **3x** **1x** **1x** **1x**

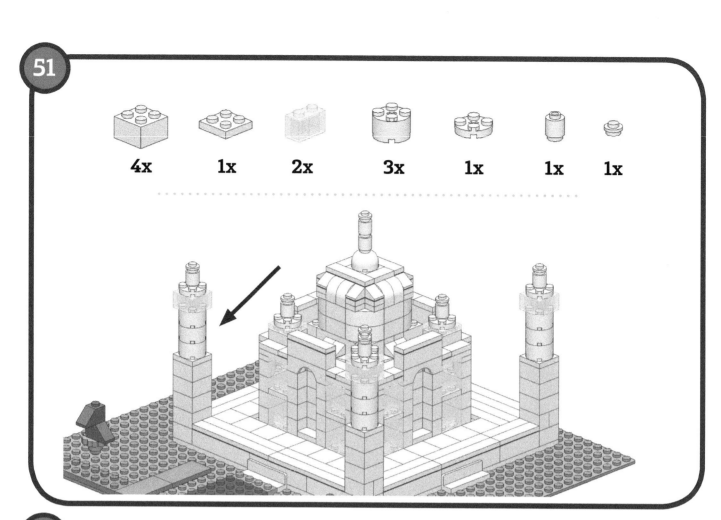

52

2x **1x** **3x** **1x** **1x** **3x** **2x** **1x**

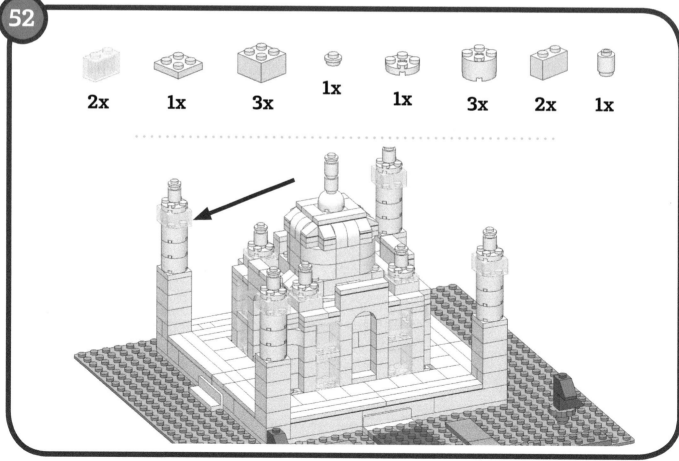

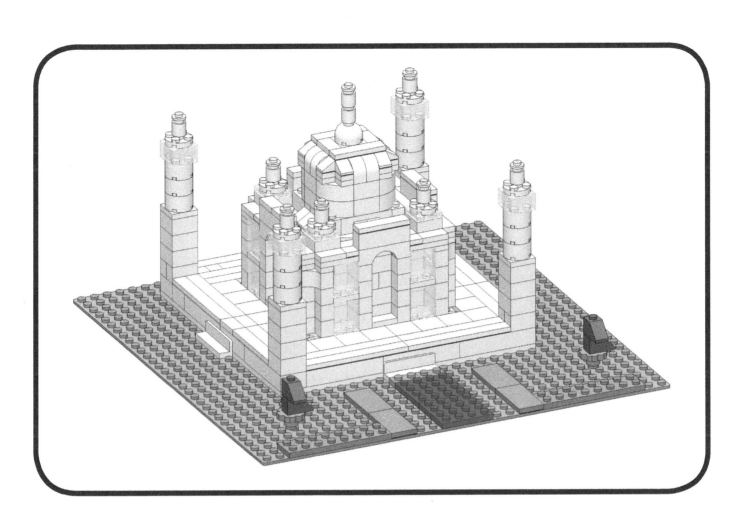

Fun Facts!

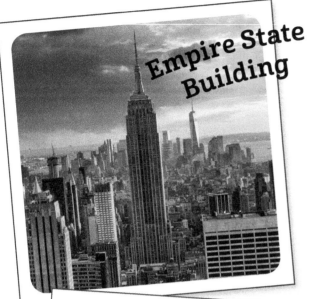

Empire State Building

- The Empire State Building is in New York, USA.
- The building took only 1 year and 45 days to build. Construction was completed in 1931, and at the time it was the tallest building in the world, at 1,250 feet. As many as 3,400 workers built the tower.
- There are about 4 million visitors every year to the observation decks on the 86th and 102nd floors.
- The Empire State Building has a lightning rod at the top that is struck by lightning dozens of times per year.
- The Empire State Building is so big it even has its own zip code.

Eiffel Tower

- The Eiffel Tower is in Paris, France.
- The tower was built in 1889 as the entrance to the World's Fair. Made of iron, it is the tallest structure in Paris, about the height of an 81-story building.
- The Eiffel Tower is named for Gustave Eiffel, whose architecture company designed the building.
- The tower is the most-visited paid monument in the world—around 7 million people visit every year.
- Every 7 years about 50 tons of paint are applied to the Eiffel Tower to protect it from rust.

- The Taj Mahal is in Agra, India.
- It took more than 20 years to build and was finished in 1653. It is made of white marble and 20,000 workers helped build it. More than 1,000 elephants were used to transport the marble.
- The four sides of the Taj Mahal are nearly identical.
- The monument was built by Emperor Shah Jahan as a memorial to his wife, Mumtaz Mahal, who died while giving birth to her 14th child.
- The Taj Mahal is the mausoleum where Shah Jahan and Mumtaz Mahal are buried.

Taj Mahal

Library of Congress Control Number: 2016946780
International Standard Book Number: 978-1-943328-83-3
978-1-513260-41-9 (e-book) | 978-1-513260-45-7 (hardbound)

Designer: Vicki Knapton

Graphic Arts Books
An imprint of

GraphicArtsBooks.com

Proudly distributed by Ingram Publisher Services

The following artists hold copyright to their images as indicated: City outline on front and back covers,
pages 1, 6-7, 21: Igor Sorokin/Shutterstock.com; the Taj Mahal on pages 38-39: In-Finity/Shutterstock.
com; Empire State Building photo, page 68: TTstudio/Shutterstock.com; Eiffel Tower photo, page 68:
Sira Anamwong/Shutterstock.com; Taj Mahal photo, page 68: Capricorn Studio/Shutterstock.com.

LEGO® is a registered trademark of the LEGO Group which does not sponsor, endorse, or authorize this
book. Disclaimer Notice: Graphic Arts Books makes no warranty, express or implied, nor assumes any legal
liability or responsibility for the accuracy, correctness, completeness, or use of the parts list associated
with a LEGO® product. LEGO Group may change the parts list of a product without notice, and Graphic Arts
Books will not be liable to anyone in respect of any loss, damage, injury, or expense, suffered or incurred as
a result of reliance on a Graphic Arts Books reference to a LEGO® product.

The author thanks the LDraw community for the parts database it makes available, which is used for
making instructions found in the book. For more information on LDraw, please visit ldraw.org.

Make sure your **Build It!** library is complete

○ Volume 1

○ Volume 2

○ Volume 3

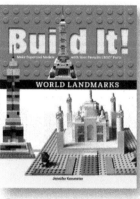

○ World Landmarks

○ Things that Fly

○ Things that Go

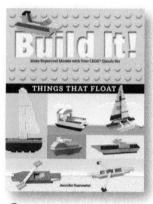

○ Things that Float

○ Robots

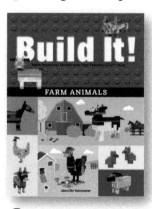

○ Farm Animals

○ Dinosaurs

○ Trains

○ Sea Life

Visit GraphicArtsBooks.com for more titles in the series